THE TRAVELS OF

GURU TEGH BAHADAR

AND

GURU GOBIND SINGH

THE TRAVELS OF

GURU TEGH BAHADAR

AND

GURU GOBIND SINGH

Translated from the original Gurmukhi

SIRDAR ATTAR SINGH

GYAN

Published by

Gyan Publishing House
5, Ansari Road
Daryaganj, New Delhi-110002
Phone: 011-47034999, 9811692060
E-mail: books@gyanbooks.com

Distribution Network
gyanbooks.com
India, USA, Canada, UK, Australia, France

ISBN : 978-81-212-9152-1 (PB)
First Published, 1876

2nd Impression 2023

Printed at: Gyan Press, Delhi.

THE TRAVELS OF GURU TEGH BAHADAR AND GURU GOBIND SINGH

Translator: SIRDAR ATTAR SINGH

THE TRAVELS OF

GURU TEGH BAHADAR

AND

GURU GOBIND SINGH.

Translated from the original Gurmukhi,

BY

SIRDAR ATTAR SINGH,

CHIEF OF BHADOUR.

January 1876.

LAHORE:

Indian Public Opinion Press by ROOKUN-UD-DIN.

CAMP AGRA, 26*th January* 1876.

SIR,

I am directed by His Royal Highness the Prince of Wales to acknowledge, with thanks, the copy of the book which you have been so good as to send him through His Honor the Lieutenant Governor of the Punjab, and which has been graciously accepted by His Royal Highness.

I remain,

Sir,

Yours very faithfully,

(Sd.) H. B. E. FRERE.

To

SIRDAR ATTAR SINGH,

OF BHADAUR.

PREFACE.

These Sakhis were originally written in a very crude language, intermingled with poetry. Through them we become acquainted with the origin of the Seikh religion; the manners and customs of the Seikhs; and many of their prophecies bearing upon political and ecclesiastical matters. Such prophecies are always found scattered through their historical books, as in the Hadis of the Mahomedans, and are the main sources of the errors into which they have been often led.

To Government a book like the present, is no doubt of great value; and, being myself duly impressed with its importance, I venture to offer it for the gracious acceptance of His Royal Highness, the Prince of Wales.

SIRDAR ATTAR SINGH,

OF BHADAUR.

LAHORE,
The 17*th January* 1876.

THE NATURE OF THE SEIKH PROPHECIES.

Injustice, tyranny, and misrule, are the main sources of commotions; but as these disturbing agents have vanished under the present administration, which has introduced laws and regulations suited to the age, and to the altered condition of the country, having refrained from interference in religious matters, far greater peace and tranquillity, than existed at any former period, have been secured. There should have been no mutinies under such an administration, and a continuous peace should have reigned over the country; but we find that disturbances have taken place. These are to be attributed to the religious prejudices of the people, by whom the very tolerance of the government is regarded as a hardship. The old prophecies affect their minds to such a degree, that they are often tempted to strike for freedom. Without multiplying instances, it will be sufficient to mention the mutiny of 1857, and the recent Kuka outbreak.

The ignorance of the people, the tolerance of the government, and the jealousies and suspicions arising out of antagonistic creeds, have often endangered the country. Designing men prompted by the extravagant assurances of prophecy have often lured their countrymen to destruction, and impregnated their minds with an undying hostility to their rulers.

Religion itself appears to have lost its hold upon men's minds, for we find many endeavouring to establish new religions, but the old prophecies still maintain their ground, and will yet lead to important changes.

These prophecies, however, are mere fabrications, as I shall endeavour to show. Shrewd men without any supernatural powers, are often able to scan the probabilities of the future ; and those under their influence, prompted by faith, often take such steps as in the end naturally bring about the fulfilment of their predictions. Mahomed, for instance, inculcated that crusades were highly meritorious, and at the same time predicted that his followers would always prove victorious if they fought bravely. Their faith in Mahomed was so great that they invariably fought well, aud thus caused the fulfilment of an uninspired prediction. In this way men were often deluded into the belief that their self-made prophets possessed supernatural powers.

The way in which Ram Singh Kuka established himself as a prophet is also worthy of notice. The 51st Sakhi of the Sakhi Book contains the following :—

"*Ram Singh uth Neuchan dare thue ek Risondee kare;*" *i. e.,* Ram Singh will rise ; men of low caste will be afraid of him ; he will introduce equality into the world.

It is recorded that Guru Gobind Singh on one occasion addressed a servant named Ram Kour, or Ram Singh, as follows : 'Ram Singh, a low caste will rise to power, and rule without fear.' Predictions to the same effect may be found in all the Shastars, where it is distinctly stated that in the present Kalijug, matters will gradually go from bad to worse, till a base caste becomes paramount. Ram Singh Kuka simply modified this prophecy to suit his own ends.

Another interpretation is that the lion of Ram, *i. e.*, Ram Singh, will become the ruler of this country; that his position will at first be endangered by men of low caste, but that in the end he will triumph.

It will be at once seen that these indefinite words may be made to refer to any one that happens to be called Ram Singh; and thus it is that whenever a Ram Singh makes himself prominent in any way, this prophecy is at once supposed to point to him. Ram Singh Kuka had therefore no difficulty in making his followers believe that he himself was the subject of the prophecy.

Another passage of the same nature, is to be found in the 15th Sakhi. It is as follows :—

'*Rilpoor beech Badhee soot hai, Bullia Raj kariga sae;*' *i. e.*, 'In the village of Rilpoor there will flourish a carpenter's son, who will reign by force of arms.'

The word Rilpoor ought to mean Rawal Pindee, and the words 'carpenter's son' would then point to the Ramgharrias, a family of Seikh carpenters who possess extensive estates and are growing richer every day. But no Ramgharria Sirdar has hitherto paid any attention to this prediction. If they attached any weight to it, it would be easy for them to collect a large body of followers. Ram Singh Kuka, however, interprets the words in his own favour, and has succeeded in inspiring his ignorant followers with a firm belief in himself. He represents himself to be the true Ram Singh, because he is a carpenter, and as for Rilpoor, he finds no difficulty in proving that it means Raya Bhani, his own native village.

Although the passages I have quoted occur in different Sakhis, still, interested and designing interpreters bring them together to suit their own purposes. It may be well questioned how Rilpoor can mean Raya Bhani, there being no resemblance between the two words ; but unprincipled men are not over nice : the words begin with the same letter, and that they know will suffice to delude the ignorant.

Predictions, it is well known, have often turned out true by chance. Those regarding Daleeb Singh were evidently uninspired, but still the course of events has led the vulgar to consider them fulfilled, as they have not the sense, or the knowledge, which can alone enable us to judge in such matters. Examine the Sakhi book, and it will be at once clear, that events have turned against Ram Singh, but still the mass of the people continue to believe in him.

These prophecies are mysterious and vague, and are well calculated to deceive the people.

If the Kuka sect is not suppressed, its doctrines will spread, and lead to outbreaks far more violent and serious than the last. The Sakhi of Sohava has made a deep impression upon their minds, and from all I have heard there is every probability of another attempt to realize the assurances therein given.

At Sohava, as indicated by the prophecy, a large peepul has already overspread a jund, and is enveloping it more and more completely every day. The time is therefore drawing near, and of this the Kukas feel so sure, that they often go to Sohava to watch the progress of the peepul. 'Alas!' they exclaim, looking at the trees, 'the peepul has not yet fully covered the jund. Hira Singh and others disobeyed our Guru in being too precipitate, and brought all this misery upon us. But our Guru is infallible. When the peepul covers the jund completely, he will return to India and conquer it.'

This story of the jund and the peepul is evidently a recent fabrication. It must have been written by some fanatic who was shrewd enough to perceive that the peepul would eventually spread over the jund tree. It is open to suspicion, even if we admit that Guru Gobind Singh was its author, for he must have seen that nothing was more probable than that the peepul would sooner or later destroy the jund. The Guru's followers were increasing rapidly, and simply needed a stimulus to urge them to daring deeds. A prediction of this nature was well calculated to awaken their energies, and to inspire them with hope. There is nothing surprising in the fact of their believing it, for does it not promise them the sovereignty of the country. One peculiar feature of the credulity of the Seikhs is, that they can never conceive how a prediction may be accomplished by chance, or in the ordinary course of events, without being inspired. They never care to notice, that while scores of predictions have turned out false, only one or two have proved to be true.

In 1823, Bahadar Singh, a zamindar of Bhadaur, a man of the same stamp as Ram Singh Kuka, gave himself out to be a prophet. He built a tank at Athur, a village in the Tahseel of Jagraon, and called it Ram Sar, or Ram's tank. Annual fairs began to be held there, and people flocked to it in great numbers. He was taken prisoner in an attack on Bhadaur, and sank at once into oblivion. His prophecies were no longer heeded, and no one looks forward to their fulfilment.

It would be well for the Seikhs to profit by the

sad experiences of the past. So many impositions have been practiced upon them, that it is high time to become cautious. The prophecies of Surbung in 1857 have all turned out false, but the Seikhs have not yet opened their eyes; they are still in fact willing to be deceived.

The Sakhi Book gave rise to a revolt in Lahore in favor of Daleeb Singh, during the Seikh regime, but its predictions turned out false, and the book was set aside as unreliable and worthless. However, it has regained its hold upon the credulity of the vulgar; and to it we must attribute the recent Kuka outbreak. The masses of the Seikh population are too ignorant to be trusted; they are liable to be led astray by designing men; and it behooves the government therefore to be vigilant.

A perusal of the legends contained in the Sakhi Book, cannot fail to be of advantage. There is no doubt that the Seikhs will continue subject to the same influences as hitherto, and their past history, therefore, will, I think, be the best guide to the statesman.

SIRDAR ATTAR SINGH,

OF BHADAUR.

TRAVELS OF GURU TEGH BAHADAR

AND

GURU GOBIND SINGH.

MAY THE SRI SAT GURU BLESS THE WRITER.

Sakhi 1.

Guru Tegh Bahadar intended that the account of his travels should be read by pilgrims for their guidance in this vale of tears. In accordance with the wishes of his faithful and devoted disciples he set out on a pilgrimage, and, after the first stage, halted near a well at Saif-Abad,* a place as charming as Panch Buttee.† Sharf-din, the chief of this village, was a good hearted gen-

* A town 4 miles to the east of Patiala, now called Bahadar Gurh, in which there is a pucca fort.

† Hindu Faqirs build huts called Buttees on the banks of rivers.

tleman. Hearing of the Guru's arrival he was overjoyed, and waited on him with presents consisting of excellent fruit, and furnished him with supplies. Addressing the Guru he said, 'O honored Guru, you have blessed me.' The Guru replied, 'You have set your thoughts on God, and therefore you and yours shall be blessed for 21 generations.' Sharf-din asked the Guru to put up at his palace, but the Guru replied that he was very comfortable where he was. Leaving some servants to wait upon the Guru, Sharf-din returned to his palace, where he prepared separate apartments for the Guru and his honored lady, who had accompanied him. The arrangements being at last completed, Sharf-din went to the garden in which the Guru was encamped, and pressed him to remove to the apartments prepared for him. Accepting the offer, the Guru set out on horseback for the palace, accompanied by Sharf-din who walked at his side, while the Guru's lady followed in a covered palanquin. On arriving at the gate of the town, the Guru's eyes fell upon a mosque, and Sharf-din immediately said that that was the house of God, but that the place prepared for his reception was a few steps further on. When the Guru arrived at his destination, Sharf-din presented him with gold-mohars, and robes, and made an obeisance to him, while his wife likewise made an obeisance to the Guru's lady and presented her with several articles of dress, and ornaments.

The Guru asked Sharf-din why he had built his house there, and Sharf-din replied that the spot was an auspicious one, for he once observed, while out riding, some wolves in pursuit of a sheep with a new born lamb, and both escaped unharmed. The Guru remarking that the walls of the building were not sufficiently thick, Sharf-din asked him to make them thicker, but the Guru rejoined saying, that one Karm Singh would, at some future period, increase the breadth of the walls and re-name the place in honor of the Seikhs. That he would build shrines both inside and outside, and also build his tomb.

The Guru then retured to his camp in the garden, but his wife and her brother Kirpal, and several other Seikhs, remained behind. When Sharf-din came to see him one day, the Guru said that he was preparing to depart, as the rainy season had passed away. 'Your presence here,' said Sharf-din, 'was a source of great pleasure to me.' The Guru advised him to fix his thoughts on God, to minister to devotees and saints, and to be humble and lowly in heart, for then he would be always happy. Sharf-din from that day adopted the style of a mendicant, and lived like a recluse in his own house.

At his departure, Sharf-din presented the Guru with cooking utensils, tents, a camel, and a splendid horse, as well as a carriage for his lady, and asked him where he intended to go. The Guru told him that he was going to the 'jungle country' in which was situated the Seikh 'Kanshee,'* though unknown up to the present time. 'I am now going,' said he, 'to make it known to the world.' On being pressed, the Guru promised to visit him again on his return, and then mounted his horse as Sharf-din held the stirrup. He encamped that day at Lang.†

* The Dumdama Sahib.

† Lang Chalalan consists of two villages 10 miles to the north-west of Patiala.

Sakhi 2.

Baba Gurditta, the ornament of. Seikhism, who gave us souls and bodies, should always be worshipped.

When the Guru arrived at the village of Mulowal in Patiala, he asked for water, but some zamindars, who were sitting near a well, said, that the water was brackish, and that the well was in consequence covered over with branches. The Guru ordered them to remove the branches and to bring him some water. After washing his face, and rinsing his mouth, he declared the water to be sweet, and since then the water of that well has become sweet, as is well known. The Guru then predicted that other wells would be sunk at that place. The zamindars now cover up every tenth well in this part of the country. The Guru having encamped to the west of the village, enquired about the principal inhabitants, and was informed by Gobinda Chowdri that there were seven headmen in the village, but that he was the only person who received and entertained travellers. The Guru then expressed his intention of giving turbans to all the headmen. He halted there nine days, and the villagers were very attentive to him.

Sakhi 3.

At the next stage his horse suffered from a severe colic, and he was obliged to halt. The place at which he stopped is still held in great veneration.

Sakhi 4.

The Guru continued his journey the next day, and halted at the village of Sekha, in the Patiala territory, near an old temple, round which there were formerly 22 villages, inhabited by Jats of the Jowanda clan.

Tuloka, the chief of this clan, was celebrating his daughter's wedding at the time with great pomp. He gave 22 feasts to his son-in-law's followers, but took no notice of the Guru, who was hospitably received by Durgoo Hurceka of the Sidho clan or 'got,' whom the Guru blessed, being much pleased with him; but he was extremely enraged with the Jowanda tribe.

It is said that Guru Gobind Singh was with Guru Tegh Bahadar on this occasion.

One day Tuloka wore shoes embroidered with

silver, and was seen by the Guru, who made enquiries about him. They told him that his name was Tuloka. 'He is mentally blind,' said the Guru. When told that he was the possessor of 22 villages, the Guru clapped his hands and said three times, 'All are gone, neither 22 nor 23 remain.' The Jowandas were the followers of Madho Dass Bairagi, whose son-in-law was living in this village, and had at one time served the Guru, who now advised him to return to his house in the Jallandar Doab, as the Jowandas were about to the destroyed like the Syalpoors. He therefore removed to the Jallandar Doab with his family.

Sakhi 5.

The Guru then proceeded to Addihaya in Patiala, and halted under a grove of Tahli trees. When the Jowandas afterwards heard of the curse pronounced upon them by the Guru, they hastened after him and entreated him earnestly, saying, 'O protector of the poor, forgive us, we have gone astray.' The Guru said, 'O Jowandas, you will not be allowed to dwell in your village, but in any other place where you may settle, you will prosper.' The Jowandas of Koombhurwal in the Patiala territory having come to the Guru with milk, and other provisions, he was much pleased with them and blessed them, saying, that their village would continue to prosper. Esa Khan's army subsequently attacked and destroyed the Jowandas, but the inhabitants of Koombhurwal, who had presented the Guru with a horse, were saved by his blessing. Afterwards a village sprang up about a mile westward of the spot where the ancient temple of Sekha stood. Joga Singh of Hareeka, who knew that the Guru had put up at Mulowal, though he was not sure at what particular place, began to make enquiries, and an old shoe-maker pointed out the Kareer tree under which the Guru had placed his couch. Joga Singh built a small platform there and used to prostrate himself regularly before it. The Pathans became hostile to him, but he never discontinued the practice of bowing before the platform. He became the chief of Sekha, where his decendants live to this day.

The inhabitants of Addihaya also took no notice of the Guru, and he was very much displeased with them. A certain farmer was very much annoyed at seeing the Guru's herdsman grazing his cattle on the pastures, and putting a scarf round the neck of the offender, dragged him away. The man complained to the Guru of the treatment he had received, and it soon after happened that the people of that village began to die of swollen necks. The Guru, who was living under a tope of Tahli trees near a small tank, was waited upon by a zamindar, who having made his obeisance sat down, and began to describe how the people were dying of swollen necks. The Guru said that they must have persecuted some Seikh. 'O Guru,' said the zamindar, 'the devastation is great. A lad who brought his wife home only yesterday, died to-day.' The Guru said, that they would recover by bathing in the tank, and when the zamindar objected that shoe-makers washed leather in it, and that it was filthy, the Guru himself bathed in it, and took some mud out of it. When informed by the zamindars of this circumstance, the whole village came to the tank to bathe, and made the water quite muddy. The plague disappeared from the village, and the people began to enjoy health. Even up to the present day, the people of this village resort to this tank in cases of sickness, as is well known throughout India. The people then began to minister to the Guru, who, being propitiated, asked to what caste the zamindars living there belonged, and on being told that they were of the Sarao caste, he said that the village would prosper.

Sakhi 6.

The Guru then marched on to a place within a mile of the village of Dhoula in the Nabha territory. The Guru's horse suddenly stopped here, and became so obstinate that he would not move. The Guru whipped and spurred the animal, but he only backed a little, and again stood still. The Guru thereupon remarked that the villagers were the slaves of the Mohamedans, and that therefore his horse would not proceed. He returned to the village of Sohewal, and made a 'Socheta' there.

Sakhi 7.

The Guru did not stop at Kalla, because the people of that village did not receive him hospitably.

He did not halt even at Bussiyan, which is situated in British territory, but pitched his camp at a village near Dhilwan in Nabha territory. The zamindars inhabiting that village were called 'Motas.' An eclipse of the sun took place that day, and the Guru performed some magnificent ceremonies on the occasion. The crowds of religious mendicants assembled there were fed by the Guru, who also distributed 101 Kupla cows, which are considered the best. The Goojraties of Tuppa, a village in the Patiala territory, at first declined to receive the cows, but after some explanation from the Guru, accepted them. In the evening the Guru started, and made a 'Socheta' at Doolwein, which was inhabited by people of the Dhaluval tribe, for the village of Mour did not then exist. There is a tank near this village, and those who give alms there during an eclipse prosper exceedingly.

SAKHI 8.

The next halt was at Dikhan, a village in Bhadour territory, where a Seikh entreated the Guru to come to his house. He had no issue, and therefore pressed the Guru very earnestly. The Guru prayed for him, and he got children. After entertaining his guest for many days, he and all his family became disciples of the Guru.

SAKHI 9.

The Guru encamped the next day at the village of Maisar Khana, in the Patiala territory, and the day after at Pandherin, where he went to a Dharmsala, and ordered his attendants to enquire for a place to put up in. The Jats pointed out a potter's house, where they said strangers were generally received. The Seikhs called the people of this village fools, and the Guru turned his horse to continue his journey, whereupon Khomari Chowdri remarked that these strangers were very proud.

SAKHI 10.

The Guru halted the next day at Ali Sheri, and the people of Bhunder hearing that Guru Tegh Bahadar had passed them without halting at their village, were extremely grieved, and said among themselves, 'It is a matter of great regret that the Guru stopped at the village of Dhilwan for three months, and we did not entertain him even for a single day.' They came to Ali Sheri in great anxiety, bringing with them a present consisting of an eight anna piece, and two lumps of jaggery. Enquiring on the way whether it was necessary for visitors to make a present to the Guru, and being told by some one that it was optional to give or not to give, and that he himself had visited the Guru without presenting anything, the people of Bhandar ate up the jaggery, and dividing the eight annas among themselves, visited the Guru empty-handed. When the people of Ali Sheri heard that the Bhandars had given no present, they followed their example, and also visited the Guru empty-handed.

The trunk of a plum tree, which had been severed from its roots, was lying near the platform upon which the Guru put up. This dry trunk suddenly brought forth leaves and branches in answer to the Guru's prayers.

SAKHI 11.

On the following day at noon, the Guru having halted at Joga, a village in the Patiala state, asked whether any one lived in that neighbourhood, and was told that very few people were to be seen there. He then marched further on, and met Jograj who begged of him to stay at his house. The Guru advised him to build a village there, as it was an auspicious spot. Jograj accordingly founded the village of Joga. The Guru then halted at Bhoopoli, a village in Patiala, and the people there supplied him with milk and cream, and grass and gram for his horses.

SAKHI 12.

The Guru then marched onwards and halted at Kheewa, in the state of Patiala, where only one Seikh named Singha visited the Guru, and supplied him with grass, fuel, and cooking utensils. When he wanted to return to his house, the Guru said, 'Why are you going so soon, sit down.' Singha represented that a zamindar's son had been betrothed that day, and that sugar was being distributed in the village, and that it was therefore necessary for him to go. 'You are appointed,' said the Guru, 'to my service ; stop here, and you will be allowed double rations.' Singha remained as directed, and enjoyed double rations.

Sakhi 13.

The Guru on his march to Sinaka, a village in the Patiala territory, met a body of Seikhs from Kabul. He halted at once, and spread his carpets under the trees of a forest. They sung some hymns, and made their offerings, and the Guru being much pleased blessed them. A zamindar, who was ploughing his land near that place, observed what was going on, and thinking that he must be some great man, placed bread and butter-milk before the Guru, who handed them to his disciples, saying, 'This is your share, and you may enjoy it.' After eating a little himself, he blessed the zamindar, and said, that milk would always abound in his house; and so it happened.

SAKHI 14.

He next marched to Bhikhee in Patiala. Three days after, Desoo, a resident of this village, came with presents, and the Guru, said, 'Come Desraj, sit down here. Why have you put your staff aside?' Desoo replied that he was a worshipper of Sakhi Sultan, and carried the staff as a symbol. 'How is it,' said the Guru, 'that you being a Hindu, worship Mahomedan saints. Cast away this staff. I have conferred a kingdom upon you.' Presenting him with five arrows out of the quiver of the 52 'Beers' or departed heroes, he added, 'I have given you 5 arrows of the bravest Beers. You will be victorious wherever you go. If you remain a Seikh, you will become a king, but if you are faithless, you will perish.' Desoo bowed and returned to his fort.

The Guru after making another stage, halted at Khisla in Patiala.

The Shaikhs or disciples of the prophet Sarwar came to Desraj and said, 'Behold you have committed a great sin in throwing away the staff, and paying heed to the words of the Shodhi, Guru Tegh Bahadar, who is nothing more than a sorcerer. Repent now, and prepare an offering for the prophet. Throw away the arrows, and resume the staff. Bow down before it, and keep it always with you.' Throwing away the arrows in compliance with this admonition, Desoo resumed his staff, while the disciples of Sarwar broke the arrows into pieces, and threw them into an oven. Thus did Desraj ruin himself at the instigation of the disciples of Sarwar.

SAKHI 15.

A Brahman waited on the Guru at Khiala, and after a little while when he was going, the Guru ordered him to send some fire. The Brahman brought fire, water and milk ; the fire being borne by a boy, the water by a woman, and the milk by himself. As they stood with these presents, the Guru gave some milk to the Brahman and his boy, and to many other Seikhs, and blessed the Brahman, saying, 'You will always receive fees at Rajput weddings and milk will abound in your house.' The Guru further declared that a well would be sunk, and a 'bir' tree planted at that place. This actually happened afterwards.

SAKHI 16.

The Guru next stopped at Mour, a village situated on the boundary line between Patiala and Nabha. In searching for a resting place he observed a large enclosure with a 'jund' tree in the middle, and asked the people of the village to open the door that he might put up there.

The Lumberdars, however, begged earnestly that he would not do so, as the place was haunted by a demon, who would kill any man or woman that went there, for only a few days ago a child had been killed by him. The Guru said he would drive out the demon, and cause a pure spirit to take his place. 'I do not fear demons,' said he, 'I have already driven one, with all his companions, out of Anundpur, and am quite able to drive this one away also.' At night the demon told the Guru that about 145 years since he was expelled from Goindwall by Guru Amar Das, and had taken up his abode in that wild country. The Guru, however, ordered him away to some other place, saying, 'I consider Tulwandi as sacred as Benares, and no evil spirit shall be allowed to remain within twelve miles of it. Depart, I advise you, for a god will take up his abode here, and the people of this vicinity will beeome as virtuous as gods.' According to the Guru's directions, a 'peepul' tree sprang up in the place of the 'jund,' which was destroyed. The villagers then placed implicit faith in the Guru, and served him faithfully during his sojourn amongst them.

SAKHI 17.

At Mour, the Guru used to go every day to a tank and make the villagers clean it in his presence while he sat under the Tali trees. The anniversary of one of the eight preceding Gurus having fallen during his residence here, the Seikhs and devotees from all quarters came to see the Guru. After a month and ten days, while arranging to proceed on his journey, he fell into a trance, and remained unconscious for many days. When he recovered, multitudes of villagers and Seikhs came to make enquiries. He told them that the five Beers given to Dessoo had been treated very badly by him, and that they had therefore destroyed him. The villagers pleaded for Desoo, saying, 'He is related to us, for Bheekha's daughter is married to Bugga, the son of Sukhia Rai. Let us bring him to you.' The Guru told them to make haste ; but when they went aud urged Desoo to come, he would not listen to them. Fate is inexorable and no one can evade it. Desoo did not appreciate the Guru's gift. 'I exalted Desoo,' said the Guru, 'to a position lofty enough to make him worthy of the name of Desraj, and he would have become the possessor of a flourishing village in this barren land, but he has now forfeited my favor.' The Seikhs of Mour continued standing before the Guru as supplicants, and he again asked them what they wanted. 'Honored master,' said they, 'is the whole nation of Châhuls to be destroyed for the fault of one man?' 'I have forgiven the nation,' rejoined the Guru ; 'they shall remain in peace and safety, and many of them will become Seikhs. I withdraw my curse ; I forgive for the sake of the Seikhs, and will protect every man in the nation, except Desoo who shall be utterly destroyed by demons.'

Sakhi 18.

The Guru next stopped at Tulwandi, where there was a mound raised by white-ants. He bowed to this mound, and his followers asked in astonishment, there being no temple in the vicinity, why he had done so. He informed them that a grand temple, nine spears in height, with golden pinnacles, would be erected on that spot. The Seikhs asked by whom, and were told that the Guru himself would appear in his tenth incarnation as a glorious being with miraculous powers, and vast wealth. 'He will,' said he, 'be both a king, and a devotee. He will give grand feasts to Brahmans, and worship the grand davi, who will remain with him always to bless him, and to make him victorious over all his enemies. He will found a third sect, he will fight great battles, and, after subduing the 22 hill principalities, will turn his arms against the Mahomedans, and spoil them of 1,000,000 horses. He will make over the government of the country to the Seikhs. He will write a new Granth. He will be born in Patna. He will live in a village, and will be victorious in a bloody battle, which will be fought about 40 miles from this place. Afterwards he will come here, and ungirdle himself and rest. I have bowed therefore in anticipation to the temple of that sacred being.' The Seikhs asked the Guru to stop there, but he said, 'No. He of whom I have spoken will sit on this spot and distribute his bounties. My shrine will be built at the foot of his temple.'

SAKHI 19.

The next day the Guru seated himself under a plum tree, and ordered his disciples to bring some spades. He took one, and with his own hands began to clear the Tulwandi tank, removing the mud five times in his own shawl. Seeing this, all who were present, Seikhs and devotees, men and women, began to clean the tank.

Sakhi 20.

'You told us some time ago,' said the Seikhs, 'that Tulwandi is your future Benares. Please explain from what indications you have come to this conclusion. Kanshi contains the temple of the god Vishaweshur Nath, and of the goddess Anpoorna; and besides these, the sacred Ganges and the Munkurnka Teerath are there.' The Guru replied that the hillock called the Dumdama was the temple of Vishaweshur Nath, and that whoever looked on it with veneration would enjoy wordly prosperity and power; would be endowed with miraculous power, and would become a true Seikh. The alms-house of this place is equal to that in the temple of Anpoorna. God's name constitutes a Ganga here, and the Gurusur Teerath is as good as that of Munkurnka in Benares. Many artists, philosophers, theologists, expounders of sacred poems, men versed in the Yoga sciences, and those who practice religious austerities, elegant copyists, students and devotees will adorn this place. I have come to see this sacred place, but the Seikhs have built no Mungi Sahib, though they expected me.

Sakhi 21.

While out hunting one day the Guru noticed a lofty structure about 5 miles away, and asked the Seikhs what is was. They told him that it was the fort of Bitunda. The Guru remarked that is was a magnificent place, and determined to halt there for nine days.

Sakhi 22.

The Guru then marched further on and halted at Soolisur, where four thieves entered his camp, two being Hindus and the other two Mahomedans. Seeing a lion crouch before the Guru, after walking round him, the Mahomedan thieves said that they would not steal any thing from the Guru as he was undoubtedly a prophet; but the Hindus said that they would, as he had horses worth thousands of rupees. The Mahomedan thieves, though they determined not to steal themselves, arranged notwithstanding to take their share of what the others stole. On unfastening the Guru's horse, which was covered with a saddle cloth, they found themselves smitten with blindness, and called to their Mahomedan companions for assistance, but they also shared the same fate. Shortly after at sunrise, the Guru hearing the noise, came to the spot and asked what was the matter. 'Protector of the poor,' said the Mahomedans, 'we came to steal your valuable horses, but seeing a lion walking round you, and crouching before you, we felt convinced that you were a prophet, and gave up the idea of stealing; but our Hindu companions unfastened your horse and became blind. On coming to their assistance we also became blind, and at day-break the Seikhs arrested us and brought us before you.' 'Why were you going to take the horse away at night? Take it away now,' said the Guru. 'O Sir,' said the thieves, 'we are but as grass before you. Condemn us to the punishment prescribed for thieves.' The Guru sentenced them to death, and they were made to walk through the branches of a 'jund' tree. The thorns killed one of the Hindus, but the other thieves were released.

SAKHI 23.

The Guru marched next to Barhai in Patiala,

and advised the inhabitants of that place to remove to another locality where he said they would be safe from their enemies. For four months the rainy season detained the Guru at this village, where he fed his cattle on green gram which he had previously caused to be sown.

SAKHI 24.

He stopped at Wuchhohana, in Patiala, for seven days, under the shade of a 'peepul' tree, near a large tank. Multitudes resorted to him here, and brought buffaloes, which supplied the Seikhs with milk, and buttermilk. Among these there was a brown buffalo which gave a great quantity of milk. When the Seikhs praised it, the Guru said, 'This buffalo will never cease to give milk.' The village was inhabited by the Rungher tribe.

SAKHI 25.

The Guru then marched to Gobindpoor, where the Seikhs were very attentive to him.

SAKHI 26.

The next day the Guru halted half way to Gogi, and reached that place the day after. When his servants went to bring grass for the horses they were beaten very severely by the Runghers and the Burghassias. The Guru being very angry, prepared to leave the village, and though the Runghers begged for forgiveness and entreated him to stay, he would not overlook their offence.

SAKHI 27.

The next day the Guru halted at Goorna, where the Jats of Goga followed him, but he took no notice of them.

SAKHI 28.

On the following day, the Guru halted at Makoror, where he was also followed by the Jats of Goga, whom the Sungat now recommended to mercy, saying, 'O protector of the poor, although these Jats have committed a heinous crime, still we trust you will pardon them now.' The Guru replied, that he had pulled up their roots, and cast them into the sea. The Sungat's influence, however, prevailed so far that the Burghassias were pardoned.

Addressing the Goolgoolia tribe, the Guru said, that five of their number would be able to stand against the whole of the Syodvian tribe. On the other hand, the Syodvians were told, that their power would never exceed moderate limits.

The herdsmen of the Sidhoo tribe were in attendance with blankets and jars of ghee. The Guru accepted their presents, and confirmed their faith in Seikhism.

Sakhi 29.

At Jheend the next day the Guru met one of his Musunds, a zamindar named Duggoo. 'Duggoo,' said, he, 'for meeting me here with this present, milk shall abound in your house. Minister to the Seikhs and devotees, and remain with us during our stay in this place.

The Guru then ordered his followers to wash his clothes in the adjoining tank, for they had been soiled in crossing the Ghaggar in a boat on the previous day. At the same time he desired them not to wash any petticoats there, as it was a sacred Teerath. When the Seikhs asked what Teerath it was, he told them that it was the place where the famous heroes Tâoo and Kussoo fought, and where the great Rama gave his grand feast; that, Nuthoo Khatri having repaired it, and restored the images of the gods to the ancient temple, it was now called Nuthoowana; that Medni Mull zamindar used to distribute food to the poor after bathing in this tank; and that, his wife, who also used to bathe here, finding the tank dry one morning, and being very much disappointed, prayed that, if it were really sacred, it would supply her with sufficient water to perform her devotions, and that immediately upon her lifting a clod, water gushed out and filled the tank; and that, since that day, no one washed bed clothes in it. Thus all became acquainted with the importance of this Teerath, which since that day has been called Gooroosur, while the place at which the Guru's clothes were washed is called Dhoba.

Sakhi 30.

Bhai Phairoo Oodassee, the Guru's old waterman, had served Guru Har Rai and Guru Har Kishn in that capacity. He was so thoroughly devoted to his duties, that he never allowed himself leisure to open his big turban, and comb his hair, which consequently was full of vermin. One day, while he was making his salaam, a louse fell out, and he picked it up and replaced it in his hair. The Guru asked why he acted in that strange manner. 'Protector of the poor,' said the man, 'this louse became homeless, and I simply restored him to his dwelling.' 'Ask anything you please,' said the Guru in astonishment. 'I am,' said the man, 'but the slave of your slaves, and want nothing except your prayers to keep me from want.' 'O Bhai Phairoo,' said the Guru, 'you shall never be in want, and, moreover, as you have served in the kitchens of three Gurus, you shall have a kitchen of your own to feed the poor. You shall be the father of a clan, in which even mendicants shall be rich, for the Guru's service is not unprofitable. O Bhai Phairoo, you are honest, and your devotion is perfect. You will overcome the troubles of this world. The true Guru is very much indebted to you.'

SAKHI 31.

One day the Guru seeing a woman sweeping the ground, asked who she was. She replied, that she was Ekadshi, in whose honor a fast is strictly observed by all Hindus of the Vaishnav caste. 'We believe in one invisible God, and cannot enjoin the observance of this fast, but still do not prohibit its observance. In this place, a great fair will be held annually on the Nirjala Ekadshi, and many people will keep the fast.'

SAKHI 32.

The Dewali festival was now approaching, and the place began to be crowded by multitudes of Seikhs and saints. Karah Pershad and other delicacies in large quantities were prepared and distributed. 'Many Seikhs from all quarters,' said the Guru, 'will come to our shrine in the Bânjar country, but very few natives of this part of the country will be converted to Seikhism. A large fair will be held annually at this place on such occasions. Drums will be beaten, the holy Granth will be read, sacred hymns will be sung, banners unfurled, horses and elephants will be drawn up in array, and bread will be distributed to the poor who will be called together by a proclamation.' 'Protector of the poor,' said the Seikhs, 'we have seen the jungle country, the future Kanshi of the Guru, and the Bânjar country; let us now see Koolchaiter, where the famous battle between the Kairans and Pandans was fought.' The Guru replied that he intended to remain there for 15 days more to celebrate the anniversary of Baba Nanak at the next full moon, and that afterwards he would proceed. He accordingly ordered fire places to be built near his tents to prepare food for the Brahmans and saints. He asked Missar Tajee Mull what delicacies he preferred, and the Missar recommended Kheer,—milk and rice boiled together and mixed with sugar,—but at the same time stated, that Baba Nanak's favorite dish was Karah Pershad. The Guru ordered both to be prepared, 'For,' said he, 'a grand Yag was given here by Maharaja Ram Chander Jee, and this is the anniversary of Baba Nanak.' A large quantity of milk was therefore procured, and Kheer, Karah Pershad, Puries and Kuchowries, were in preparation for 24 hours. On the following morning the Brahmans and saints were assembled and seated in rows to partake of the banquet. Indeed, all who came that day were welcome. Such was the Yag of Baba Nanak's anniversary. The Guru's name is still remembered there in connection with this magnificent feast.

Sakhi 33.

The gold mohars were given to the Musund Duggo to sink a well for the Guru, and to clear the tank, as he was the proper man for this work, being a zamindar of the village. The Guru moreover warned him to be honest in the matter, as the money had been raised for charitable purposes, and any misappropriation would lead to his ruin as it had to that of many other great men. Duggo, however, did not act honestly. He made the well on his own estate, and not in the place indicated by the Guru. The shaft collapsed, and another well which he made was ruined in the same way. Moreover, Duggo's family which consisted of 18 members perished within a very short period, and he had no one left to perform his funeral obsequies. Akh plants sprang up on his hearth, and he was totally ruined, as is well known to all. Duggo himself shortly after died, and Bhai Tahldass, a disciple of Bhai Phairoo, was appointed in his place.

SAKHI 34.

The Guru next encamped at the junction of the Markunda, the Surusotee, and the Ghugger, near the village of Khanowree, which is now in British territory. Matung Rishi, an ancient devotee, having practised religious austerities at this spot, it is as much venerated as Tribanee, which is now called Sangam.

SAKHI. 35.

The Guru next halted at the village of Bahirjukh in Patiala, at the house of a carpenter whose affection for the Guru was so great, that he carved a magnificent throne and canopy for him. This throne he worshipped by burning incense, and lighting a lamp before it every day. He would not leave his house for fear of thieves, and hoped the true King would come to his house some day and bless him. The Guru now sat upon this throne, and the carpenter who was overwhelmed with joy, washed his feet with water, of which he and the members of his family drank. The Guru gladly made him a Seikh, and said that Seikhism would flourish in his house.

The Seikhs then asked the Guru to explain the word 'Jukh.' He replied that in the famous battle of the Kairuns and the Pandans, four Jukhs were posted so as to prevent any one from running away from the field. Their names were Bahir Jukh, Ram Jukh, Rattan Jukh, and Tirkhoo Jukh.

It was on this occasion that Dilsookh said, 'Protector of the poor, how foolish have I been in devoting myself to the welfare of my relatives who do not care in the least for my happiness, and would be ready, even during my life time, to divide among themselves the property which I have acquired, and guarded with such assiduity. The body is like a house, and our senses, *viz.*, hearing, seeing, smelling, feeling, and tasting, like five thieves, are plundering it day and night.' 'Dilsookh,' said the Guru, 'true happiness consists in meditation, and not in riches or seclusion. He who devotes himself to prayer day and night is as holy as a god himself; and Guru Nanak says, that there is no difference between him and a god. This doctrine of Nanak's should be firmly believed. He who sets his mind on God is free from want, and, though he lives in the world, is a deserving man.' The people asked whether he would come to their village again, and he said that he would visit the place once more.

Sakhi 36.

The Guru moved on to Kythal the next day, and encamped at Dhundhar Teerath. The people of the city came to see him, and among them there was a young carpenter who invited the Guru to put up at his house, as it was in danger of being robbed that night. The Guru said that he did not fear robbers, and would prefer to stay there.

They wanted to know what days the Guru reckoned sacred, and he mentioned the following :—

1. Baisakhee, or the first day of the month of Baisakh.
2. Dewali.
3. Maghee, or the first day of Magh.
4. Every full moon.
5. The tenth day of every lunar month, as Baba Nanak was born on that day.

Besides these, any other day upon which devotees and holy men assemble to worship God, is to be held sacred.

The Guru and his Sungat are like the warp and woof in cloth,—there is no difference between them.

The young carpenter prepared Karah Pershad, and many other kinds of food on the Dusmi day, and the dishes were so numerous that no one could think of any that had been omitted. The Guru and his wife, convinced of the sincerity of his faith, came to the carpenter's house with a large number of their attendants. They all sat down in the courtyard and on the terrace, the Guru being placed on a stool covered with silk. Bhai Gurditta of the Ramdass caste read the Anand, and then the food was served. After dinner the Chulli was read, and the young Seikh, having made some offerings to the Guru, put his head on his feet and said, 'Honored Sir, protector of the poor, I am your slave.' 'Excellent is your faith, young man,' said the Guru, 'your house will be a stronghold of Seikhism. Religious books will be read, and sacred songs will be sung for ever there.' The Guru then returned with his attendants to Dhindar Terath.

Sakhi 37.

Starting from Kythal, the Guru halted at Barna, where a faithful Seikh supplied him with provisions, and begged that he would come to his farm, where a surveyor had been sent by Government to value his crops. 'Your presence,' said he, 'will make him show me some consideration.' 'Stand at my side,' said the Guru, 'and have no fear, for by my miraculous power the surveyor will not be able to form any estimate of your crops.' The surveyor tried his best, but could not measure the field, and at last was obliged to ask the Seikh to tell him its area. The man said 125 bigahs, but the surveyor told him that he had measured it three times, and found it to be only 25 bigahs. When the Seikh remarked that this was owing to the Guru's favor, the surveyor asked to be presented, and was introduced to the Guru, before whom he bowed, asking why he had not been able to measure the field. The Guru replied, that like the words on a seal, the decrees of fate are written in reversed characters on the forehead of every man, but that they became straight when he bowed before the Guru. 'Protector of the poor,' said the surveyor, 'I forego even the 25 bigahs, provided you make me your Seikh.' The Guru consented, and made him a convert.

Sakhi 38.

The Guru then resumed his journey, and on arriving at Raja Karn's Hill, stopped his horse, and said, 'Behold what a great man Raja Karn was. He gave away a maund and a quarter of gold in charity every day, and even parted with his own skin, when asked to do so.' The Guru halted here, and gave a grand feast to the Brahmans. He afterwards visited Sidh Buttee, or Baba Nanak's tomb, as well as Guru Hargobind's, and after performing the usual ceremonies at these sacred places, gave a public feast to the Brahmans, who, having asked him to provide for their children and grand children, were presented with a Hookumnama, or general order, engraved on copper, directing his followers to supply their wants.

Sakhi 39.

The Guru arrived the next day at a village which the zamindars told him was called Kharola. The Guru told them not to call it Kharola but Rukhwala, the guardian.

The lumberdars of Jullal now visited the Guru, and presenting him with coarse sugar, two pitchers of milk, and a beautiful spear, asked him to pray that they might be victorious over the people of another village which was hostile to them. The Guru was pleased with the spear, and blessed them, saying, that, if they continued humble and faithful, they would be victorious. 'Those who attack you,' said the Guru, 'shall be defeated, and their boasting shall be turned to shame.'

The Guru then employed some Burars, as he had done on a previous occasion.

In Sumbat 1825, the zamindars of Jullal attacked the Guru's camp on a dark night, and after killing two Seikhs, ran off with five of his horses. The next morning the Guru's men attacked and overcame them. The lumberdars after paying the usual fine, called Tunkhawah, and providing Karah Pershad, begged for pardon, saying, that the Guru had ordered them to be humble and faithful, but that they had disobeyed his injunctions. They built a village near the Guru's camp, and called it Gurusur.

Sakhi 40.

Leaving this village, the Guru arrived at Bhugta,

a village now in the Faridkot territory, and seating himself near a well under a 'pepul' tree, enquired by whom the well had been made. On being told that it had been made by Bhugta, he said, the proverb of the Emperor's wealth and the soap-maker's name was applicable. The Seikhs wanted further explanations, and the Guru related the following anecdote :—

Ramoon, the prime minister of King Mohdan, had a daughter who was possessed of a devil, and came to the Guru to have her cured. The Guru ordered him to fall at the feet of Bhugta, who was then sitting at the Guru's side. He did so, and Bhugta blessed him, and said, 'Your daughter is cured.' The devil immediately left her, and entreated Bhugta to let him go, promising to be of some service to him when required. Bhugta therefore released him. Ramoon offered to reward Bhugta, who asked him to make a well for him in his village. Ramoon accordingly built the well, but it collapsed as soon as it was ready, owing to the magical arts of Kalian Dass Bairagee, who had also sunk a well previously in that village. Bhugta now summoned the devil whom he had released, and commanded him to repair the well. With the assistance of other devils, who were in his service, he procured stone from Delhi, and lime from Lahore, and rebuilt the well in one night. Bhai Bhugta now built a fort, and announced that he had reserved one side of it for the devil. He also ordered five maunds of gram to be provided daily, and the people used to hear the devils grinding it. A large quantity of flax was also spun by them every night. These circumstances are well known to all the residents of Bhagta.

Sakhi 41.

At the village of Bhugta, an armed Seikh accompanied by his son, a little boy, presented him with a basket of boiled corn. He asked the boy his name, and was informed by the father that he had not yet been named. The man asked the Guru to give him any name he pleased, and the latter after performing the Pauhal ceremony, named him Ghoongna Singh, with reference to the boiled corn.

The lad wanted to go with the Guru, but his father told him that he was as yet too young to enter the service of that personage. He promised, however, to make him over to the Guru when he was old enough. After making a present of 2 Rs. 8 annas, the Seikh took his leave, and returned to his house.

Sakhi 42.

The Guru then left Bhugta, and arrived at Bandar, in the Faridkot territory, and halted there. The Seikhs who accompanied him, finding that the village was called Bandar, which means a monkey, remarked in jest that it was a village of monkeys, but the Guru told them, that Bandar was the name of a Gôt, or clan of zamindars. The inhabitants of this village supplied the Guru with provisions during his stay there.

Sakhi 43.

The Guru next encamped at Bungari, in the Faridkot territory, and the inhabitants supplied him with provisions, and showed him every consideration. His followers called his attention to the wild looks of the natives, and he informed them that they were robbers, free and subject to no rulers ; that they lived by plunder ; but that now, as he had come among them, they would reform and be of some service to the Seikhs in future.

SAKHI 44.

The Guru next marched from Bahbul to Shivram where he addressed the Burar clan, saying, 'O Burars, if you act bravely and courageously, we will overcome the Mahomedans. Enter my service, and I will pay you handsomely.' 'O King,' replied the Burars, 'we can plunder property worth thousand of rupees, and return to our homes every evening.' 'You can continue to plunder the Mahomedans, and remain in your homes,' said the Guru, 'but simply submit to my control, and obey my orders. I will put you into the way of obtaining booty.' 'Then, we will be your subjects,' replied the Burars, 'and will always fight your battles.' Thus the Burars always mustered strong round the Guru, one party relieving another.

SAKHI 45.

The Guru halted at Shivram, and met a white-bearded Syad, dressed in white, who had concealed himself under a 'sareeh' tree, near the Doda tank. The Syad saluted the Guru, who enquired if he was well and happy. 'Yes,' replied the Syad, 'I am really happy now, having seen your divine countenance.' The Seikhs asked who the man was, and the Guru told them that, during his life time, he had been a virtuous and pious man, but having had a great love for the 'sareeh' tree, he was now confined in one.

The villagers supplied the Guru with provisions, but as he was accompanied by a large number of Seikhs, it was arranged, that the men should be billeted in the village. A very poor man, who could not even provide for his own daily necessaries, was also asked in jest by the zamindars to entertain a Seikh. Feeling ashamed to decline the honor, he took the Seikh to his house, and spreading his cloak for him to sit upon, washed his feet with warm water. Having no bread, he procured some dry berries from a 'peeloo' tree, and boiling them in water, placed them before his guest. After eating and washing his hands, the Seikh took leave of his poor host, and returned to the Guru's camp, the poor man accompanying him a part of the way, till he was made to go back. When all the other Seikhs had returned to the camp, the Guru asked each of them what he had eaten. One said bread and butter-milk, another bread and cream, while others said bread and ghee, kichree and ghee, and so on. When the poor man's guest was asked what he had eaten, he stated that he had partaken of some very excellent and delicious food. How the poor man, being so destitute himself, could have given such excellent food to the Seikh, was a matter of surprise to all. The Guru therefore sent for the poor man, and asked him what food he had given. After some hesitation, he declared that he had given nothing beyond a cup of water; but on being pressed still further by the Guru, he candidly acknowledged that he had given nothing but dry berries. The Guru was deeply impressed with what he heard, and exclaimed, 'Excellent is Seikhism, and blessed are the Seikhs. The Guru would willingly lay down his life for the man who is content to eat whatever his poor host can set before him. If the rich man provides inferior food, he is a sinner, but when a poor man prepares a plain meal, and his guest declines to partake of it, the sin falls upon the latter.'

SAKHI 46.

The Sakhi of Kapura.

At Kote Kapura, a village in the Faridkot territory, the Guru sent Bhai Dyal Singh to call the Lumberdar Kapura, who immediately obeyed the summons, and brought an excellent horse, with which the Guru was very much pleased. Two days after this Kapura again came to the Guru dressed in a long robe, which hung down to his feet. As he was approaching, the Seikhs remarked that he was covering the Guru's weapons with dust.

Kapura lifted his long robe, and bowing to the Guru, indignantly took his seat on one side. After a while, he asked why the Seikhs were waving fly-brushes over the arms, and was told that it was being done to keep off the flies. The Guru now addressed him, saying, 'O Kapura, let us make war against the Mahomedans.' Kapura replied, 'O Guru, we are not strong enough to cope with them, for why were you not able to conquer Anandpur, your own village. The emperor will hang us if we rebel against him.' 'Yes Kapura,' said the Guru, 'the Mahomedans will tie bags of filth to your mouth before hanging you, and your descendants will beg from door to door.' In fact, the Guru became so angry that he broke up his camp and departed.

A few days after Kote Kapura was sacked by Esa Khan Munjh, and Kapura, who was found hiding in a hay stack, was brought before Esa Khan, who said, 'You keep hawks and cocks Kapura, why did you hide yourself like a cock.' The Mahomedans carried him away with them, and upon reaching a tank in the desert, hanged him. When the noose was placed round his neck, he asked them to allow him to bathe and tie a bag to his mouth, before being hanged, 'For,' said he, 'if my Guru's prediction is not fulfilled, I will be born a second time, to suffer and to die again.' They accordingly tied a bag of filth to his mouth, and hanged him. The Guru, however, was pleased with Kapura's brother Hameera, for he was obedient and submissive. He retained the Pergunnah of Bungara, which had been conferred on him.

Sakhi 47.

The Guru proceeded on his journey, and stopping at a hillock near the village of Jaitoo, in the Nabha territory, began to amuse himself by discharging arrows. 'What village is that I see yonder,' he asked of Khana, who, as he could not see it, said, 'What village? Those are merely the huts of some Jaitoos of the Khana caste.' But the Guru persisted, saying, 'No brother there is a large village yonder.'

Halting at Jaitoo, he went out hunting alone one day, and in the heat of the sport, proceeded to a spot between Kotha Prithi Chand and the village of

Mulooka, in Bhadour territory, where he ordered his tents to be brought.

SAKHI 48.

About two hours before sunrise, a man named Dewana, whose head and beard were shaved, came to the Guru's tent, and asked for an interview. The door-keeper told him that it was not the proper time, but that he would be admitted in the morning. Dewana, however, insisted. Being told that the Guru was engaged in meditation, and could not be disturbed, struck the door-keeper with a wooden pestle, and wanted to rush in by force, but the door-keeper wounded him with his sword. Two hours after sunrise, Dewana again asked permission to see the Guru, who ordering him to be brought in, asked if he wished to live. 'No, my Guru,' said Dewana, bowing, 'permit me at once to breathe my last in your presence.' He obtained his wish, and all the chiefs of the Jungle were astonished and alarmed at his fate. Some turned against the Guru, and the faith of others was confirmed. 'What kind of a Guru is this,' said the Burars, 'who kills a Dewana,

Some, however, asserted that the man was only a servant, and had been killed by the Guru's orders.

The Guru passed through the village of Chamtra and returned to Jaitoo. He declared that the tank at Jaitoo was a grand Teerath, and superior even to the Ganges.

Sakhi 49.

The Guru next halted at Soniur, which was inhabited by the Dogar tribe. Here a man named Shama brought milk and all his buffaloes to him.

While out hunting one day on the plains, the Guru was saluted by Kapura. 'Are you well and happy Kapura,' asked the Guru. 'No Sir, I am not at all happy,' replied the man, 'ever since you left my village in displeasure.' The Guru presented him with a sword and a shield ; but, notwithstanding this honor, he still declined to fight for the Guru, who, thereupon, said, 'Begone Kapura, you will be a coward.'

Sakhi 50.

The Guru next halted at Ramiana, in Patiala

territory. Seeing a zamindar picking something from the wild shrubs, he asked him what he was doing, and on being told that he was gathering 'dela' berries, ordered the man to bring them to him. The zamindar gave him a handful, but finding them bitter, the Guru ordered them to be thrown away. The man threw away a quarter of what he had, and on being told to throw the rest away also, parted with another quarter. The Guru repeated his order, and the man only threw away another quarter, and then insisted on keeping the remainder, saying, 'Sir, what will my children eat.' 'Beware,' said the Guru, 'you are retaining a fourth part of the famine which is raging in your country. If you had thrown the whole away the famine would have ceased altogether.'

Further on the Guru met Jograj of the Barung family, a resident of Ramiana. His followers told this man that if the Mahomedan soldiers enquired, he was not to tell them that the Guru had passed that way. He promised not to tell, but shortly after, when the soldiers came, and asked if he knew anything of the Guru, he told them that he had just passed, and that his followers had enjoined him not to tell. The Guru hearing of this treachery, cursed Jograj, saying, that he would die of a swelling in his stomach. This curse was fulfilled, and his descendants to this day die in the same way, after lingering three days.

Still further on, the Guru met Rupa Khatri, who presented a lump of jaggery. The Guru wanted to put up at his house, but he refused to receive him, saying, 'Sir, I cannot entertain you at my house, for the emperor will destroy me and my family. Do you wish to destroy me?' 'Behold,' said the Guru, 'you and your family shall be destroyed, but this village, though it may be laid in ruins many times, shall always be rebuilt.' The village was indeed destroyed, and rebuilt 30 years after, but no trace can be found of Rupa's descendants.

Sakhi 51.

As the Guru was riding along, a young Barar, the son of Dan Singh, came up and whipped his horse, saying, 'O headstrong chief, fly as fast as you can, for the Mahomedan troops are approaching to attack you.' Turning round, the Guru said, 'May your offspring be destroyed. Why did you whip my favourite horse?' Dan Singh pleaded for forgiveness, saying, 'Honored Guru, we Barars are great fools, and prone to sin, but you are a merciful master. We often give utterance to what is improper. Pray forgive my son. Like a terrible black serpent you are able to destroy any one that thwarts you. You have cursed and destroyed Shumshera and Kapura who did not obey your orders. I am the slave of your slaves, forgive my son, for I am your humble disciple.' The Guru relented and said, 'Dan Singh I forgive. The curse pronounced by a father upon his son has no effect.' 'What token have I,' said Dan Singh, 'of your forgiveness.' 'A lioness,' said the Guru, 'catches her whelps in her mouth, but does not bite them.' Dan Singh fell at the Guru's feet, and then took his leave.

SAKHI 52.

Further on, while crossing a desert, he felt thirsty

and called for water. The Seikhs searched everywhere, and at last found that a man named Rai Khana had some water in a leathern bag. They asked for some, but Khana, after denying that he had any, at length offered to sell it, asking a rupee for each cup. The Seikhs agreed to give this, but he drew back, demanding a gold mohur for each cup. The Guru's treasurer agreed to give him even a gold mohur, and they brought a cup of water to the Guru, who hearing of the circumstances under which it had been obtained, cursed Khana, saying, 'You shall become thinner than water, O Khana.'

SAKHI 53.

The Guru passing by Mookutsur, stopped on a hillock, where one of his followers, climbing a 'mâl' tree, saw some Mahomedan troops, about two miles away, approaching them, and informed their master accordingly. 'Their eyes are filled with dust, and their mouths closed with a hard wooden plug. Their eyes shall be opened, but they shall not be able to see.' A body of Seikhs from the Majha country threw a sheet on a bush and hid themselves. In the meantime the Mahomedan troops arrived, but could not find the Guru. A Seikh, followed by five others, jumped out of the bush, and attacked them. Five more now sallied out to assist their brethren, and in this manner, five at a time advanced, till 40 of them fell, and obtained the crown of martyrdom. They killed 250 Mahomedans, for the Guru himself discharged an arrow, which made a dreadful noise, and caused the earth to tremble. A woman also fought with a spear.

The Mahomedans at length retired, thinking that the Guru had been slain. The troops being parched with thirst, their commander asked whether there was any water in the vicinity. Kapura said, 'O Khan Jee, water is only procurable at a place 10 miles in our rear, or at another 30 miles further on.' 'What is to be done,' said the officer, 'we are dying of thirst?' Kapura advised them to go back on their horses, as fast as possible, to the place where water was procurable. The Mahomedans having to bury their dead hesitated, but Kapura suggested that they should strip the dead of their arms, and leave them on the ground, as that would amount to the same thing as burying them. 'Procure water for yourselves,' said he, 'you have been victorious; it is not well to allow the troops to perish of thirst.' 'Kapura is wise, let us follow his advice,' said the commander. He was the Governor of Sirhind, which had been cursed by the Guru, against whom he has come with 5,000 horse and foot. After a long pursuit he had at last succeeded in bringing him to action. From that day the Mahomedans never ventured to fight with the Guru. After the departure of the Mahomedans, the Guru came down from the hillock to the battle-field, and wiping the faces of his wounded followers, conferred upon them the titles of Dus-Hazaries, Bees-Hazaries, and so on, according to the number of paces each had advanced against the enemy in the battle, such being the practice of the Mogul Emperors. Coming up to Mahan Singh, who was dying of his severe wounds, he enquired if there was anything his Guru could do for him. 'I have seen the Guru's face,' said Mahan Singh, 'and have nothing more left to desire.' But when the Guru insisted on his making a request, he simply asked him to heal the wounded. 'O Mahan Singh, ask something else,' said the Guru, 'for it is difficult to grant this request.' 'If you are favorably disposed,' resumed Mahan Singh, 'grant me this single favor. I do not want anything else.' 'Excellent is the Khalsa,' exclaimed the Guru, and Mahan Singh immediately expired.

SAKHI 54.

A Seikh woman came to the Guru asking him to pray that she might have a son. She had given up all her wealth and comforts, and become a mendicant. She was in the Guru's camp when the battle took place and had been wounded. 'You fickle creature,' said the Guru, 'you came here for a son, and now you have become a mendicant!' When her wound was healed she began to go about naked, but the Guru ordered her to wear a 'Kuch' and a 'Pecha.' Mai Bhago, for that was the name given her by the Guru, adopted this dress, and moreover armed herself with a javelin, weighing a maund and a quarter. She became very pious, and devoted herself entirely to God and the Guru. She always remained in the Guru's camp, and used to guard his bed with ten other Seikhs, who were under her orders. All respected her as a goddess, and the Guru was highly pleased with her. 'Mahan Singh did well,' she used to say, 'in only asking the Guru to heal the wounded.'

SAKHI 55.

There were many withered 'mâl' trees on the plain where the battle had been fought, and the Guru ordered them to be collected to form a large funeral pile for the 40 Seikhs who had been killed. Setting fire to the pile with his own hands, he sat down under a 'mâl' tree, and said, 'These men are saved, and have attained the dignity of holy devotees and saints.' Arti-Sola, or the funeral service, was then read, and after Karah Pershad had been distributed, the Guru consecrated the spot, saying, 'This place, and the shrine of the Mookta martyrs, shall be equal in sanctity, and those who worship here shall obtain the blessings they seek.'

Sakhi 56.

The Guru continued his journey, and encamped at Sarai near a tank, on one side of which there lived a devotee. This holy man enquired who had pitched his camp on the opposite side of the tank, and was told by his disciples that it was the Guru who had lately fought with the Mahomedans. The devotee then asked his age, and being told that he was only 35 years old, exclaimed, 'What can I expect from him if he is only 35 years old.' These words were spoken in the presence of some of the Seikhs, and they repeated them to the Guru, who simply observed that the devotee was proud of his age. The Seikhs asked how old he was, and were told that he had lived 1,120 years, and was well versed in the Yoga sciences. This being mentioned to the devotee by his disciples, he remarked that it was astonishing to find so much knowledge in one of the Guru's age. He took up his staff at once, and came to the Guru, whom he found engaged in evening prayer. The devotee stood till he was invited to a seat, and when the prayers were over, conversed for some time, and at last offered to become a Seikh. The Guru replied, that he was already one, and needed no conversion. The Guru was highly pleased with the devotee, who again remarked that he was astonished to find such knowledge in one so young. 'Devotee,' said the Guru, 'you have retained your old garment, but he who receives a new one wears it.'

The Seikhs asked the devotee how many famines he had seen in his life time, and he said, that, on rising from his meditations on one occasion, and finding no one about him, he set out from his hermitage. That after going three stages, he met a man who told him that a dreadful famine had been raging in the country for 12 years, and that there had been no rain within a radius of 500 miles during that period. That the price of a goat's head had risen to 50 Rs., and that the inhabitants of the country had consequently perished to a great extent. The devotee then took his leave, and returned to his dwelling.

Sakhi 57.

The Juts of the Hureeke clan did not allow the Guru to halt at Nowthea, a village in the Patiala territory.

Sakhi 58.

The Guru proceeded on his journey, and halted at the village of Futta Summoo, where the Hureeke farmers presented him with a Khase and a Loongee. When he bound the former round his waist, and put the latter on his shoulders, a Seikh who was sitting by, appeared astonished, but the Guru reminded him of the proverb which inculcates, that the dress should suit the country, or, in other words, that a man should adopt the prevailing fashion wherever he goes.

The Guru ordered the Hureeke farmers to watch

his camp at night, but they told him that there was no fear. The Guru insisted, but they would not admit the necessity of doing so. He again urged them, saying that his Seikhs slept very sound after intoxicating themselves with Bhung, and that the Burars in his service being as bad as dacoits, it was absolutely necessary for them to watch the camp. They therefore ordered the Dogars who were in their service to watch. When a quarter of the night had passed, the Guru enquired if any of the Hureeke men were awake. The guard replied that they were Dogars. Repeating the same question twice during the night, and receiving the same reply, he said, 'Behold they to whom the lot has fallen shall receive the reward. Live and prosper O Dogars, I make you the headmen of this village.' The Dogars then approached, and prostrated themselves before the Guru.

Sakhi 59.

The Guru next encamped in a forest under a large 'bir' tree.

Sakhi 60.

The day after he halted at Wuzeedpur, a village near Kussur. 'Yonder is Kussur,' said the Seikhs, 'where there are 22 nobles at whose gates bands of musicians are always in attendance.' 'A time is coming,' said the Guru, 'when music shall resound in my village, Kahna Kacha.'

Hearing the call of a partridge, he remarked, 'We know you by your voice,' and mounting his Arab, he set his hawk and hounds on the bird, but it hid itself in the thorn bushes for a long time, and after a harassing pursuit of nearly 25 miles was at last taken. The Guru at once ordered it to be plucked and thrown to the hawk, which began to tear off its flesh and eat it alive. Dan Singh Aspal, seeing this, said, 'O cruel chief, who can blame you, but you have uselessly fatigued your horse for a poor partridge. Such a persevering pursuit after a lion would have been justifiable. In a few minutes we could have killed many partridges in the adjoining jungle.' 'Dan Singh,' said the Guru, 'there is no scarcity of game, but I had particular business with this partridge.' 'What special business,' said Dan Singh, 'could you have with this partridge. Protector of the poor, you have dealt very severely with it.' 'Dan Singh,' continued the Guru, 'this partridge was a farmer in his previous existence and owed some money to this hawk, which at one time was a Bunya, or rather a Khatri. Not being able to pay the debt, he fled. After two or three years the farmer came to this village on some important business, and was seized by the Bunya, who determined not to let him go till his money was paid. The farmer begged hard, promising to pay every pice at some future time. The Bunya demanded a security, but the farmer having no other friend, said, he would get the Guru to stand security. 'I agree,' said the Bunya, 'but you must act honorably.' The farmer proved dishonest, and the Bunya, though he released me from my obligation, was bent on prosecutiug his claim against the debtor. I have therefore made over this partridge to the hawk to be torn in pieces and devoured.' Dan Singh then rose, and fell at the Guru's feet, saying, 'Forgive my impertinence.' 'It does not matter,' rejoined the Guru, 'you only asked a simple question.' Dan Singh bowed and took his leave.

On this occasion the Guru put three pegs of jund wood into the ground. These became large trees which are worshipped by the Seikhs to this day.

SAKHI 61.

The Guru arrived the next day at Muktsur, which is now in British territory,—(May the Guru protect us. May Guru Gobind Singh Rai enable us to overcome the difficulties of this world). The Guru here declared, that a battle field is as sacred as the soil of Kurcheter; for as in Kurcheter it is not necessary to collect the bones from a funeral pile to cast them into the Ganges, so it is not necessary to remove the bodies of the slain from a battle field. A battle had been fought at Muktsur by the Seikh Martyrs, and he therefore ordered his tents to be pitched here.

Sakhi 62.

The Guru then marched to Roopiana where he drank bhung, and shot a crow with an arrow. Zora Singh asked why he had killed the bird, and he replied as follows :—'This bird has come into this world a hundred times, as a crow, and was once a Sheikh Raja. A poor Seikh invited him to dinner on one occasion, and he accepted the invitation. He came on the day appointed, and happening to see the Seikh's daughter, who was very beautiful, fell in love with her. At night he sent his servants to fetch her away from her father's house. Seeing the men at his door, the Seikh was very angry, but the girl pacified him, and asked him to accompany her to the Raja's palace. She excused herself that night, promising to return on the following night, without being sent for. The Raja agreed, but warned her not to play any trick. 'What trick can I play,' she said, 'I will certainly come to-morrow.' On returning to her own house, the girl poisoned herself; and in her last moments said, 'The Raja is a villain and a crow.' In consequence of this curse, the Raja continued to be a crow during a hundred births.'

SAKHI 63.

During his stay here, a Jogee, whom he had met before, came to him and said, 'You are called a Guru, shew me your power of performing miracles.' 'I will perform a miracle,' said the Guru.

On a hillock in the neighbourhood was the tomb of Bhuttee Kashub, surmounted by a beautiful dome in which the Jogee used to sit. The Guru touched this place with an arrow, bowed before it, and said, 'Are you well, Hukam Nath?' 'I am all right, O Guru,' replied the Jogee. 'This is a beautiful place,' continued the Guru. Upon this the Khalsa demanded a fine, as he had praised a Mahomedan tomb, and the Guru acknowledging his fault, paid 25 Rupees 4 anas. 'You have,' said the Seikhs, 'made it a crime to worship tombs, somadhs and mausoleums, even by mistake, then why have you yourself bowed before this tomb?' The Guru replied, 'I have done so to introduce the practice of paying fines, and to put my law in force. This Jogee asked me to perform a miracle, and I have with my arrow drawn away his supernatural power of coming from Delhi to Lahore, and of returning on the same day, after begging for flour.' 'Come now Hukam Nath,' said he, addressing the Jogee, 'let us travel from Delhi to Lahore.' 'You have deprived me of the power. I cannot do so now,' said the Jogee.

On the spot where the Guru halted there are three jund trees, whose trunks have grown into each other. They are worshipped, and vows are made before them to this day, for the Guru suspended his weapons on their branches.

The Jogee used at first to send a servant with a basket of wild fruit, which sufficed for any number of persons that happened to be present ; but he no longer possessed the power to perform this miracle.

The Jogee's calves used to go about loose among his cows without touching their teats, but now they began to drink up all the milk. The Jogee used to boil 'Khichree' in an earthen pot, which being thrown upon the ground, divided into as many plates as there were persons present. But now when he had occasion to resort to this miracle, the pot simply broke into two or three pieces. Thus all the supernatural powers of the Jogee were lost, because he had ventured to try the Guru, by asking him to perform a miracle. He fled with his cows to Ruttia, leaving the rest of his property, consisting of horses, carts, mills, clothes, and utensils, behind him.

Sakhi 64.

While he was out hunting one day, the Guru came to the village of Bhoondur, which was six miles from his camp. Bhoondur, the owner of the village, presented him with a piece of cloth and 5 Rs. in cash, giving milk and sugar to the Seikhs at the same time. Bhoondur, moreover, offered the Guru his services, and entreated him to make some stay, but, after a little conversation, the Guru rose to depart, and returned to his camp through the village of Therie.

SAKHI 65.

The Guru next halted at Kal Jhuranee. There was a nest full of raven's young ones on a Pholahee tree near this village, and Dharm Singh was ordered to go to this nest and kill the first long necked raven that he met. He went, and Prem Singh who was standing under the tree at the time, witnessed the deed. The Seikhs hearing of this, said, 'Protector of the poor, you have committed a great act of violence.' The Guru explained as follows :—'This young raven was my cook formerly, and used to be very harsh to my Seikhs while distributing their food. They called him a raven, and said in jest that he cawed like one. I have now given him salvation.' The Seikhs then prostrated themselves, and thanked the Guru for his mercies.

At the Kantiawala tank, which is situated to the west of this village, the Guru saw a large serpent coming towards him, and killed it with an arrow, remarking that it was formerly a Musand, who was so proud, that he would never bow to any one.

Sakhi 66.

The Guru halted at Gooroosur, where the Sadhees entertained him, and supplied him with provisions. He used to go out hunting and riding followed by a crowd of Burars, who talked idly on various subjects.

Sakhi 67.

The Guru next halted at Chhutliana near the hillock of a mendicant named Wahmee. Here the Burars laid hold of his horse's reins, saying, 'Give us our wages, or we will not let you proceed.' The Guru promised to pay, but the Burars said, 'You have been evading payment in this way for many days; but now as you are approaching the villages of the Sobas, we will not let you move, until you pay us.' 'Will you have Seikhism or your wages,' said the Guru. 'We will much rather have our wages, and do not care for Seikhism.' On this the Guru discharged an arrow upwards, and the sky becoming clouded immediately, heavy rain and hailstones began to fall over a radius of one mile all round. The Burars fled and hid themselves under the Mal trees, leaving the Guru, who remained seated on his horse. The Seikhs covered the animal with blankets, and the Guru further protected him by placing an arrow on his head.

After some time, when the storm had cleared away, the Guru casting a pitying glance towards the Burars, saw among them a Seikh, who, coming up to him, asked where he should deposit the treasure which was laden on his mule. Ordering the treasure to be brought before him and opening the sack, the Guru found that it contained a great heap of rupees and gold mohurs, and at once ordered the pay of the soldiers to be distributed at the rate of 8 annas a day to a horseman, and 4 annas a day to a footman, there being 500 of the former and 900 of the latter. The Guru offered Dan Singh his salary, but he refused saying, 'O true king, let me only be a Seikh. I have plenty of wealth and property.' 'Dan Singh,' said the Guru, you have preserved the seeds of Seikhism, from which it will again spring up. Why do you not wear long hair on your head?' 'Why do you desire it?' asked Dan Singh.

'He who wears long hair, and reads the Jubgee,' said the Guru,' is saved from hell, and I catch him by his long hair, and deliver him from evil.' 'You can catch me by my long beard,' said Dan Singh. The Guru laughed ; and Dan Singh agreed to keep long hair. In compliance with the Guru's order, he also received the Pauhal, but still refused to take any salary. 'Make some request of me, Dan Singh,' said the Guru, 'I am very much pleased with you.' 'Very well,' replied Dan Singh, 'if you are pleased with me come to my village.' Hunting and shooting as he went, the Guru reached a jungle, and admired the scenery. 'How far is your village now, Dan Singh?' he asked, and being told that it was a coss and a quarter further on, determined to stop where he was, as it was time to read the Lodhurs. Dan Singh provided refreshments, and his servant brought milk, which the Guru drank, and said, 'O Sooma, this is the milk of a brown buffalo.' The servant said, it was.

The next day the whole village brought the Guru Karah Pershad, and prostrating themselves before him in crowds, presented a colt. 'This jungle' said the Guru, 'is worth lakhs of rupees, let us stop here for 3 days.'

Mohna and Sooma, two zamindars, wishing to test the Guru's supernatural powers, brought the milk of a black buffalo to him one day. Thereupon the Guru said, 'O Sooma, you want to test my power ; why have you brougth me the milk of a black buffalo to-day?' Sooma excused himself by saying, 'O respected sir, my wife must have changed the milk to-day without my knowledge.' 'No,' rejoined the Guru, 'you wanted to test my power. Behold this place shall be the seat of miracles.'

Sakhi 68.

Dan Singh prepared a feast for the Guru at his own house, where the Seikhs spread their blankets on the ground, while Dan Singh served the food with his own hands.

The Guru met the Seikhs of the Jaitoo tribe at this feast ; and a charitable institution was built in his honor in the village. Before his departure the

Guru blessed Dan Singh, saying, that his house would be the head quarters of Seikhism.

SAKHI 69.

The Guru next encamped at a place which he called Gooptsur, because the Goopts, or Hindoo mystics, presented him with a large treasure here.

The Burars made merry, boasting among themselves that they had made the Guru pay them their wages by force, and a Seikh overhearing them, reported the circumstance to the Guru, who said, 'My Seikhs shall obtain a thousand times more by conquest.'

A Mahomedan Faqir of the Wahmee order who had built a tomb, 9 yards in length, with lime and pucka bricks, leaving an opening in it, on one side, large enough for him to be put in when he died, presented the Guru with a maund of ghee, a maund of sugar and the same quantity of flour. He also provided grass and grain; and moreover entreated the Guru to make him a Seikh. The Guru consented and re-named him Ajmir Singh. He had the power of performing miracles, and could collect alms in Delhi and Lahore on the same day.

Sakhi 70.

The Guru then continued his march, and met Sahib Chand with whom he drank bhung under a mal tree.

Sakhi 71.

The Guru next halted at a village called Bhai-ka-kote, where two Seikh Bunyas furnished him with provision in abundance, and became converts, being re-named Rungee Singh, and Ghomee Singh respectively. Goor Bux Singh of the Jhorur caste also became a Seikh, and presented the Guru with a stack of grass.

The forest which stood near the Guru's camp at Bhai-ka-kote is still in existence. During his stay at this village, he once went out hunting to Sooniar.

Sakhi 72.

The Guru next pitched his tents at Rohla, a village so called after the name of the barber who built it. This barber was of the Punjoo caste, and was killed in battle by Tilk Rai. The Guru stopped 9 days at Rohla, near which, are the villages of Tilkra and Bumbheea.

Sakhi 73.

At Bajak the next day, he drank bhung, and the Seikhs brought him many vessels of milk, which he distributed to his followers. One refused to drink, and when the Guru asked him why, he replied that he ate goat's flesh, and therefore did not like to drink goat's milk. He said, moreover, that cow's milk did not suit his taste, but that he had no objection to buffalo's milk. Some one said, that what he had brought was buffalo's milk. Whereupon the man willingly drank of it, when ordered to do so by the Guru.

Sakhi 74.

Two Dewana Faqirs named Gohda and Sookhoo, hearing that the Guru had killed one of their fraternity, determined on revenge and collected 50 Dewanas to attack him. Twenty-five, however, deserted in a short time, and 13 soon after, followed by 10 more, so that only 2, named Sookhoo and Boodhoo, remained. These set out with their musical instruments, a Sarungee and a Dhad, for the Guru's camp. Hiding their instruments at a neighbouring inn, they waited upon the Guru. After the usual greetings, he ordered them to produce the things which they had hid. They brought them accordingly, and being ordered to sing, tuned their instrument, and sang the following verses :—

> " Our beloved souls dwell in a frail house ;
> Our parents do not remain long with us ;
> And youth is transient. "

The Guru was preparing to mount his horse to go out riding when Sookhoo said, ' Protector of the poor, let us carry you.' Accepting his offer the Guru seated himself upon a couch, and made two Seikhs and the Dewanas carry it. As they went along he kept beating Sookhoo's bald head, while the latter imitated the sound of a Dhounsa, or drum. After going about a mile in this way, the Guru mounted his horse, for this was only a little fun which he had indulged in to please Sookhoo, in whom he found the germs of true attachment. Sookhoo now asked the Guru how he had managed to disguise himself at Machewara, and was highly amused when he seated himself on a couch, and put on the blue dress which he wore on that occasion. Sookhoo one day after prostrating himself, walked round the Guru several times, being in a trance all the while, and at last fell down exhausted and senseless. On being bathed according to the Guru's directions, he recovered, and prostrating himself, said, 'I was overpowered by divine love, O Guru; you should not have ordered me to be bathed.' The Guru presented him with a square rupee which is worshipped to this day.

SAKHI 75.

The Guru now went on to Bajak, and passed the night in a wilderness, where the Sodhees were very attentive to him.

SAKHI 76.

On reaching the tank at Jussu, the Guru rode into it, armed and dressed, as he was. When he got to the opposite bank, his blue dress, became white, the turban only retaining its color, and his black horse, also turned white, except about the head. The Seikhs being astonished, asked for an explanation, and the Guru told them, that the tank was a sacred Teerath, called Swate-Sur, and that he had entered it at the auspicious moment. That the far famed hero Ram encamped here before the battles of Lâoo and Kussoo. The Seikhs began to bathe in the tank when they heard this, but the Guru informed them, that the auspicious moment had passed. All this is well known throughout Malwa.

'We shall eat jaggery in Jussu,' said the Guru. Shortly after this speech, a trader named Lubana arrived, and presented thirty maunds of jaggery, which was distributed to the Seikhs and the horses, no other food having been prepared that day.

The Guru remained here 10 days, and received

great attention from the villagers, who, at his departure, made him such presents as they could afford.

Sakhi 77.

Starting from Jussu, the Guru arrived at Pukka, where the pegs to which his horses were fastened became jund trees, which are worshipped to this day. A platform was also built here for the Guru's bed, and the assembled multitudes shouted, 'Wah Guru.'

Sakhi 78.

The Guru continued his journey, and arrived at Dumma, where, after paying homage to the shrine of Guru Tegh Bahadar, he ordered a hillock which was situated in that vicinity to be levelled, that he might take off his armour and rest. The Seikhs gathered together, and levelled the top of the hillock, raising a small platform on it. The Guru after laying aside his armour, sat down on the platform, and declared that it had become the Dumdama of Anundpoor. 'What was it, O true king,' said the Seikhs, 'when you bowed to it.' 'It is the place,' he replied, 'where Guru Tegh Bahadar once put up for nine days, when he visited Malwa, and is therefore sacred. Prosperity and supernatural powers may be obtained here by prayer.' From that day the Seikhs have continued to venerate this shrine.

This anecdote of Guru Tegh Bahadar was related by the Guru himself.

Dulla Chowdri then presented himself, and pressed the Guru to come and put up in his fort, but he refused, saying, 'I prefer to stay outside as your women and children are living there.' 'I can remove the women,' said Dulla, 'to a separate building, or to the town. Pray do come.' But the Guru still refused, saying, that it was better to stop outside. Dulla then entreated the Guru to allow his wife at least to go and occupy the palace in the fort. He said that she was at liberty to go if she liked; but she, on being asked, said, that she preferred to remain with the Guru.

The camp was at last pitched under the walls of the fort, and all the Seikhs, except the Guru, took their meals at Dulla's house ; his food being brought out to the camp. This went on for 5 days, after which the Guru ordered all the food to be prepared in the camp. Dulla declared that he was indebted to the Guru for everything, but the latter, acknowledging Dulla's devotion, said that it was proper for the Burars to cook their own food, as they received their wages regularly.

After this Dulla entertained the Seikhs several times, and presented a horse, two shawls, and a hundred rupees to the Guru; and two superb robes, and 25 Rs., to each of his wives. He also furnished grass and gram for the Guru's horses, and provisions for his kitchen.

SAKHI 79.

The Bysakhee fair took place during the Guru's stay at this place. Many Seikhs came from all sides, some for amusement, and some from curiosity.

Ardasia seeing the enormous crowd, said, 'O king, see how many have come to seek your blessing.' 'Very few,' replied the Guru, 'have come for that purpose. The men have come to see the women, and the women to see the men. Most of them in fact have come for fun; only a few true Seikhs have come on my account.' He called a Seikh and asked him where his wife was, and the man pointed her out. He also called a Seikh woman and asked where her husband was. She pointed to the place where he was sitting. 'You see, O Ardasia,' said the Guru, 'that true Seikhs are rare.'

Another Seikh was then called and asked whether he had any relatives. He saluted the Guru, and said that he had none; that many pretended to be relatives from interested motives, but that his only true relative in this world, and in the next, was the Guru, who had given him wisdom. 'This is a faithful Seikh, O Ardasia,' said the Guru, 'and all the rest have only come together for fun. Thousands go on pilgrimages, but a few only are pious and godly; many go to battle, but the brave are rare; hundreds enter a boat in which there is only one ferryman.' Ardasia then prostrated himself, and said, 'Protector of the poor, you know all the secrets of the heart, who can hide anything from you?'

Sakhi 80.

The next day the Guru's wife mounted her horse, and went out with her attendants, consisting of innumerable horsemen and footmen, drummers, singers, and other musicians, singing and playing sacred hymns. Meanwhile the Guru sat on a platform, and favored his people with an audience, granting their requests as fast as they were made.

Sakhi 81.

The Guru was out hunting one day, when a woman called out to him, saying, 'You are Gobind, and I wish to speak to you. Your beard is superb, and your turban excellent. I belong to the Baraich clan, and my native village is Chumbha. I am going away disappointed; pray grant me a son.' 'Repeat your request,' said the Guru, and she repeated it. 'Where do you come from?' 'From Maja,' she replied. He at once called for pen and ink, and ordering her a son, handed the paper to a Seikh. 'What have you written,' asked the Seikh. 'I have ordered her a son,' said the Guru. The figure looks like 7, observed the man. 'Never mind, let it be 7,' rejoined the Guru.

Sakhi 82.

Meeting no game one day, the Guru observed that some one must have neglected to wash his hands and face, or to comb his hair. 'I have not combed my hair,' said a Seikh. 'Do it now,' said the Guru. This being done, the Guru soon made a good bag, and ruled, that before setting out on horseback, the Seikhs should always repeat the Ardas, and perform their ablutions.

Sakhi 83.

Shortly after a Seikh presented a small cup of tyre, and the Guru asked him where he came from, and whose son he was. 'I come from the village of Mour,' said the man, 'my name is Dalput, and I am the son of Bheo.' 'Yes,' said the Guru, 'you are the pride of the army. ('Dal,' meaning an army, and 'put' pride). The Guru was very much pleased with him, and bound a new turban round his head. Some musicians performed before him when he returned to his camp, and he presented them all with suits of clothes and turbans.

SAKHI 84.

Starting from Tilwandi, the Guru encamped near the village of Chak. Ram Singh, who resided there, advised him to remove the tents into the village, but he said that he preferred keeping them outside. Ram Singh then asked him to his house, and he agreed to go. Ram Singh's aunt also invited him to her house, as she was very anxious to she him. She came out to receive him, hiding her face in some cloth, which she intended to present to him. She had refused to come to Ram Singh's house, as it was surrounded by curtains, and therefore the Guru went to her house. After she had made an obeisance, Ram Singh asked the Guru to return, but he simply replied, 'I am coming.'

Ram Singh used to eat the Guru's leavings, and those of his wife were distributed by Ram Singh and his brother to the members of their respective families. The leavings of Sahib Dawan, the Guru's other wife, were thrown to the dogs, for Ram Singh's female relations refused to touch them. Sahib Dawan was offended at this, and reported the matter to the Guru, stating that it was a deliberate insult, as they had themselves asked for the leavings. The Guru called Ram Singh, and asked him to explain why they did not eat the leavings of Sahib Dawan. Ram Singh after enquiry represented that his people declined the leavings because the members of the Guru's family had not yet partaken of food with Sahib Dawan, and also because she was yet a virgin. The Guru explained, that, in consequence of a vow, he had not yet been able to consummate his marriage, and that Ram Singh's relations were perfectly justified in not eating her leavings.

SAKHI 85.

After this, Bhai Dyal Singh came with Ram Singh to pay his respects to the Guru, who, however, would not speak to him, though Ram Singh introduced him as a member of his family. Ram Singh on leaving the Guru's presence, said to Dyal Singh, 'The Guru intends to visit Bhucho to-morrow, you had better go ahead over-night and prepare food for him. He will arrive there by sunrise.'

Ram Singh presented the Guru on his departure with a bow and a pair of shawls, and Mata Sundri, and Mata Sahib Dawan, with two suits of clothes that were exactly alike.

The Guru reached Bhucho a few minutes after sunrise, and Dyal Singh begged that he would order his tents to be pitched there, but the Guru insisted on going on to Bhagoo, although Dyal Singh represented that food was ready.

Dyal Singh having refused to take the Panhal on some previous occasion, the Guru told him that he would be willing at some future time to take it from sweepers. Dyal Singh now asked for the Panhal, and it so happened, that of the five men present, four were Seikhs, and the fifth a sweeper, who was lying asleep at the time.

Dyal Singh now brought the food on carts, and, after helping the Guru and his followers, presented a horse, a pair of shawls, and a hundred rupees. About 15 Seikhs, who arrived late, reported that they had had no food, and the Guru directed them to take it by force from Dyal Singh; but he having none ready gave them his ring to buy provisions and cook some for themselves. These men joined the Guru afterwards at Bhagoo.

SAKHI 86.

He next encamped at Bathinda, where a learned Brahman, who was in his camp, told him, that, according to the laws of King Bena Pal, all kings were required to sacrifice an elephant on entering the town, because it was haunted by a demon. 'Where can we get an elephant,' said the Guru. 'Let us substitute a buffalo from some village in this vicinity.' He sent five men to bring a buffalo from Bungara, the inhabitants of which village readily offered one, on hearing that it was required by the Guru for a sacrifice. 'There is one yonder, rubbing himself against a jund tree,' they said, adding in jest, among themselves, that the animal was likely to horn them. The men went up to the buffalo and striking him with a stick, said, 'Come along, the Guru wants your head.' The villagers were surprised to see the buffalo so quiet, and remarked that the Guru must possess supernatural powers.

After sacrificing the animal, the Guru ordered the carcass to be thrown away, and Bhai Godurea offered to do so, if allowed. The Guru consenting, Godurea threw it over the ramparts of the fort with a shovel. 'You are very strong,' said the Guru, when he saw him accomplish this feat.

King Gorea had just destroyed the towers of this fort.

Godaria, so called because he always wore a quilt (godare), carried a small shawl about with him, and had planted many banian trees, being a great

Bhagat or devotee, whose prophecies often turned out true. He had followed the camp from Bhucho. 'After travelling all over the Deccan,' said the Guru one day, 'I have found, in Malwa only, a man like Godaria, who is void of avarice.'

The Guru now ordered the Chit Gupts, or spirits that register the dead, to expel the monster, who being accordingly ordered to depart, asked where he was to go. 'Go,' said the Guru, 'to one of the countries I have cursed.' When the Seikhs suggested Sirhind, the monster pleaded that he was hungry, and could not travel so far that day. The Seikhs asked how much he ate, and he told them that his quantum was a maund and a quarter, but that he had eaten nothing that day. 'You may stop at Masurpur to-day,' said the Guru, 'and go on to-morrow.'

When the Guru remarked that the fort of Bathinda was very extensive, the Barar zamindars, who were present, related that Bena Pal, while out hunting one day in that locality, saw a goat fighting with a lion, and gaining ground. Taking this as a good omen, he immediately set labourers and peasants to work to build a fort, promising to remit the revenue payable by the latter in return for their labour.

A wide subterraneous passage leads from this fort to Bhatnare.

Sakhi 87.

After leaving Bathinda, the Guru encamped at the village of Semir, and remained there all night. Dulla was admitted to an interview, and when the zamindars brought him some presents, he told them that the Guru only was entitled to receive them. 'Who am I,' said he, 'to receive any, when he is present.' 'Friendship is greater than power,' said the Guru. 'I indeed possess great powers, but it is only when I exert them, that people shew me any consideration. They have good reasons for making these presents to you.'

Sakhi 88.

The Guru next encamped at Tilwandi. There

was an entertainment that night in the village, and the ten Seikhs, whose duty it was to watch the Guru's tent at night, determined to go and see the fun. 'The Guru,' said they, 'is fast asleep, and there is no fear. Before he wakes we will be back.' Five of them went, and after a little while, feeling that they had done wrong, said, 'What have we got by coming. The Guru will be very angry. Let us return.' They came back in great fear, for they knew the Guru was equally conscious whether asleep or awake. The five who had not gone, now said, 'Why did we not go? Have not these returned after seeing the fun. We might also have returned with them, for the Guru has slept all the time.' Towards morning they went home, and when they returned to attend the durbar, the Guru asked those who went to the entertainment, as well as those who did not go, why they had absented themselves. The latter replied, that the other five only went. 'But,' rejoined the Guru, 'what did you say when they returned, and what did they say at the entertainment.' Both parties now confessed the whole truth, and the Guru remarked, 'Those who went thought of me, but those who remained, only thought of the fun.'

SAKHI 89.

During the Guru's travels in this wild country, some one informed him one day that his followers had been plundered by the Subadar; but he said nothing. The next day another came and gave the same information and the Guru remarked, 'No one has yet said that my followers have plundered the Subadar. The nine kings who preceded me, put strings of beads on the arms of their followers, but I will put swords into the hands of mine, and I will cause the hawks to be destroyed by the birds on which they prey.' He accordingly expressed a wish that all his Seikhs should carry arms, at all times; and the Seikhs have followed this injunction ever since. He then also ordered them to wear the kase, 'for,' said he, 'you can be perfect men, only by wearing the kase and bearing arms.' He, moreover, announced that he was about to train his followers to arms, and instructed Dullah the Barar to arm his troops with clubs, and plunder the Seikhs, taking care not to hurt any one, or to injure any property, because it would have to be returned, and because he simply intended to give his followers a lesson in the art of war. In the meantime he sent word to his Seikhs, that an attack was about to be made on them by the zamindars, who had revolted; and urged them to make a stout resistance, and to protect their property manfully. The Seikhs being inspired with courage, would not yield when attacked. There was a great uproar, which was heard for miles, and also reached the ears of the Guru, who was watching the battle from a distant eminence, extremely pleased with what he witnessed. 'This is the way,' said he, 'to teach the men to fight. They will conduct themselves as bravely in a real battle.'

SAKHI 90.

He now often ordered Karah Pershad to be prepared, and on each occasion directed his men to scramble for it as soon as it was ready. One day he ordered a very large quantity to be prepared, and desired his men to proceed as before. All obeyed except a few, who remained seated round him. On being asked why they did not join the rest, they replied, that they were willing to take any portion that might be given to them, but that they would not act like plunderers. The Guru approved of their conduct, but said, that amongst the Seikhs, there would be plunderers, as well as honest men. From that day nothing pleased the Guru so much as martial exercises; and the Seikhs began to worship their arms. He was not so delighted at the sight of the offerings made to him, as he was when reviewing his soldiers.

SAKHI 91.

Dullah solicited rain instead of the salary which had been allotted to him, as that wild tract of country had for a long time suffered from drought, but the Guru told him, that the clouds were not under his control. One day, the treasury being open, Dullah refused to take his allowance, and again asked for rain, but the Guru paid no heed to him.

Dullah was again asked on another occasion, when the treasury was open, to take his allowance, but, as before, he said, he would have nothing but rain. 'Husbandmen in distress, ask even the walls for rain,' said the Guru, quoting the old proverb ; and then ordered Dullah to prepare his tanks. Setting many men to work, and cheering them on with music, Dullah soon had the tanks ready, and then the rain came down in torrents, till the zamindars asked the Guru to stop it, as they had had enough.

Sakhi 92.

A Seikh told the Guru that Mula, notwithstanding his fidelity to Guru Nanak, had gone to hell, after being bit by a snake. The Guru remarked that he must have become unfaithful. 'However,' said he, 'I will make him a true Seikh, when he is born again, as he will be, in the neighbourhood of Bethinda, and in the house of a Khatri of the Tugal tribe.' 'What sign shall we have of this,' said the Seikh. 'He will,' said the Guru, 'have a lock of white hair on his head, and will be called Mula from his birth. As no one loses the reward of labor, Mula after this birth shall never be born again.'

Sakhi 93.

The Seikhs who kept watch at night, informed the Guru, that a woman used to come and stand near them, about dawn, with her hands clasped, while they slept. The Guru simply observed that it was very likely. The woman continued coming for five consecutive nights, and on the last occasion bowed her head to the ground, and retired. The Seikhs were very desirous of knowing who she was, and the Guru told them that she was Malwa, who had committed a great sin, and that she always visited him to obtain forgiveness. 'What sin,' enquired the Seikhs, eagerly. 'My dear brethren,' replied the Guru, 'Bena Pal, who built the town of Bathinda, was a very conscientious prince, in whose reign no one suffered from hunger or nakedness, so great was his charity. There were many wells and canals in his time, and he was as rich as Koonare, the god of wealth.' 'How long ago was this,' interrupted the Seikhs. 'He lived 1,400 years ago,' continued the Guru, 'and sank piles in the Sutlej, upon which he built a fort.' 'How has the fort stood so many years,' asked the Seikhs. The Guru told them that parched 'til' had been thrown into the kilns to make the bricks durable. 'A Brahman woman who lived in Bathinda,' continued the Guru, 'having some guests at her house one day, purified herself to prepare food for them. When it was ready, her child began to cry, and had a motion while she was nursing it. Covering the dirt with flour, she began to serve the Brahmans. At this the god of corn was highly incensed and went to Vishnu. 'Who has offended you,' said Vishnu. 'Who would do so. You are honored even by me, than whom there is no one more powerful.' The god of corn replied, 'He in whose country there is neither hunger nor nakedness, is greater than yourself. Such is Bena Pal, in whose dominions filth has been put to my lips.' All the gods were indignant at the insult offered to the god of corn, and Vishnu ordered Sanechur to afflict the country of

Bena Pal with famine for 12 years ; to cause the wells, the brooks, and the rivers to dry up ; and to empty the granaries in 7 days. Then Sanechur informed Bena Pal of Vishnu's displeasure, and in consideration of his virtues, advised him to leave the country. The king retired to Oojein, the capital of Bikarmadit, in Malwa. The woman you saw was Malwa, whose sin being now forgiven, the country will flourish again.' The Burar zamindars listened with great attention to this anecdote.

Sakhi 94.

Jhulan Singhi, who used to play the banjo very well, was asked by a woman servant to come in and play before the Guru's wife, as he had no listeners where he was then playing. He asked if such was her own or his mistress' wish. She replied that though she had no orders from her mistress, there was no fear of her getting angry. When informed that Jhulan Singh had come, the Guru's wife enquired whether he could play the Guru's hymns, and being told that he only played a banjo, she consented to hear him. Jhulan Singh after singing some comic songs went away, but felt very sorry for what he had done, and asked himself whether he would have sung such songs had his sister or mother been present. 'I must have given great offence,' said he. To punish himself he cut off his genital organs, and determined not to speak again. When the Guru returned and heard of what Jhulan had done, he remarked that his bad passions would never leave him. Jhulan Singh's wound healed, and he resumed his attendance on the Guru.

The site on which the village of Mour now stands, was formerly inhabited by the people of Jewand and Dulmi. Jhulan Singh and his servant used to live there in those days. The Mours from Saboo, who settled in this village afterwards, called Jhulan Singh, Aquab (the dumb man). Aquab's residence was surrounded by a forest of plum trees, and the villages of Tapah and Dhonlab Raisir were situated very close to it. Jhulan in those days was a very devout man, and, as he possessed the gift of prophecy, the Mours respected him very highly. The zamindars of Saboo at one time contemplated an attack on the Mours, and Jhulan Singh used to prevent their cattle from grazing in the direction of Tapah, by driving them back with his staff. People began to ask what Aquab meant by this strange behaviour, and continued to take their cattle out in spite of him, for they could not make out what he meant. The men of Saboo at last seized the cattle, and then it was understood why Aquab used to drive them back. As Aquab now began to strike his stomach rapidly with his hands, the Mours thought he meant that they would triumph over their enemies in the end ; and when they shortly after, with the help of their allies in a neighbouring village, brought back their cattle, Aquab became a great oracle. In fact, the house in which he lived is venerated to this day.

The Guru had predicted that Jhulan Singh's bad passions would never leave him. Whenever a wedding took place, he never failed to go and see the bride.

SAKHI 95.

The Guru made a long stay at Tilwandi, and his residence was called the dumdama, because he had taken breath (or dum) there. He had ungirded himself here, whereas his usual practice was to remain girded even while bathing.

SAKHI 96.

The Guru used often to have the 'Imrat Karah,' or the water of eternal life, prepared and thrown upon the ground. The Seikhs asked him to explain what he meant by this, and he said that the khalsa which was about to rise there, would be of a very superior order. 'This place,' said he, 'must be regarded as our Kashi. Many will study here, and become learned.'

SAKHI 97.

The Guru while out hunting one day, stopped at a place 7 cos from his dumdama, under a tali tree which was 15 cubits in girth. The people of Mour came out to him with vessels of milk, of which the

Seikhs drank, after obtaining the Guru's consent ; and then continued their journey.

Sakhi 98.

On one occasion the Guru asked his people, who was king of Malwa, when Kabir, the devotee, was alive. The Seikhs replying that they did not know, he continued, 'Does no one know him who was followed by ten lakhs of men, when they remember Kabir, the devotee. No doubt Kabir is still remembered because he devoted himself to God, and ministered to the saints. Such men will be remembered throughout the Yogas, and their memory will always be fresh. The monarchs of the world are puppets, but those who devote themselves to God, are real kings. Kabir, the devotee, should always be spoken of as Ram Kabir, for Ram and Kabir were the same.' 'Who was he?' enquired the Seikhs. 'He was called Iskandar,' replied the Guru.

Sakhi 99.

The Guru once asked his Seikhs, how the earth

was supported. 'Tell us kindly yourself,' said his followers. 'No,' rejoined the Guru, 'tell me what you have heard about this.' 'Some say,' replied the Seikhs, 'that it is supported by a bull, others that Shais Nag, the great snake, supports it.' 'Well,' said the Guru, 'I admit this, but who supports the bull or the snake?' 'Tell us yourself,' said the Seikhs. 'They stand,' said the Guru, 'upon truth. The heavens, the continents, the seas, the sun, and the moon, are all sustained by truth. Falsehood even is sustained by truth, for falsehood by itself could not exist. As iron can only float in union with wood, so falsehood is sustained by being combined with truth.' 'Right, right,' said the Seikhs, 'whatever you say is true.'

Sakhi 100.

A Seikh to whom another owed some money, and would not repay it, said, 'If you do not discharge your debt now, you will be punished at the day of judgment.' The other replied, quoting a line from some poet, 'No one demands payment after the Guru has cancelled a debt.' This conversation being overheard by the Guru, he also quoted some lines to the following effect: 'Guru Nanak has said, that debt is to a Hindu as beef, and to a Mahomedan as pork. A Guru, or a saint, cannot guarantee anything to one who feeds on carrion.' He further explained, that a Guru only pardons after a debt is discharged. 'If debts and other money transactions,' said the Guru, 'were not duly adjusted, and acquittances from the Guru were looked forward to, the world would soon come to an end. Why would men practice moderation and abstinence if they could be released from their obligations in this manner. Guru Nanak, remember, distinctly says, that all sins, except falsehood, may be forgiven.'

Sakhi 101.

Dalla entreated the Guru to explain why he ordered thousands of pens to be cut up and thrown away. 'I prophesy,' said the Guru, 'that thousands of Seikhs will hereafter study theology in this place and then pens will be mended to some purpose. This is our Kashi; those who study in this place will cast off their brutish ignorance, and rise into authors, sages, poets, and commentators. Fools even will become wise here.' 'This is very desirable,' said Dalla, 'and there is no doubt that your prophecy will be fulfilled.'

Sakhi 102.

The Guru had his dumdama, or platform, at Bathinda raised to a very unusual height, and when he took his seat on it, all his followers could see him. Whenever he bathed in the Gurusur (the Guru's tank) he called his followers to remove some portion of the mud which had settled at the bottom. Poets could not even describe the martial games in which he instructed his followers. Every evening he collected his pensioners at Jundiana, and paid them their stipends; and was so liberal, that he often gave gold mohurs instead of pice. A crowd surrounded his dumdama; Dalla and other Burars as well as thousands of Seikhs came and sat at his pure feet, for he was their prophet and the delight of their hearts. They came not from interested motives, dissimulation and hypocrisy they left behind them. They exceeded in number the multitude that attends the Anandpore fair, and it was not possible to see from one end of the crowd to the other. Songs of joy and praise were heard throughout the assembly, and all waited on the Guru, though he had his own servants. There were some who hoped to be blessed with wives and children, and prosperity. Devotees and recluses also resorted to him. Day and night the multitude surrounded him, and be daily distributed gold and silver to those who were deserving of charity, or had come to him for assistance. Drums and trumpets resounded in his durbar, like the thunder of heavy clouds. No one was admitted to a private audience till an hour and a half after sunrise ; but when he took his seat in open durbar, all viewed him with devotion. Many on hearing of the Guru from those who had been to see him, also flocked to his camp. His wealth being immense, he took hundreds into his service, and showered favors on the multitude like rain. Clothes and other articles were distributed every day. The Burars sang and danced till 12 o'clock at night. There was no room to sit where the Guru dispensed his gifts, and many were content to stand. The kings of the surrounding countries, who had rejected him before, now waited on him, and acknowledged his prophetic mission.

Dalla one day stood on guard, sword in hand, and Diala performed his part as singer in a satisfactory manner. At length the Guru ordered the former to retire as it was late, and offered to grant anything he might ask, as he felt favorably disposed towards him. Dalla putting his hands together, said, 'All I want is to be allowed to sit at your feet. Wherever you may be, keep a small place for me.' 'Dalla,' said the Guru, 'drink of the Imrat (the water of eternal life), as the other Seikhs have done.' 'I have,' said Dalla, 'often done so.' 'When,' said the Guru. Dalla replied, that the Guru's leavings, of which he had often eaten, were to him as the Imrat. 'O Dalla,' said the Guru, 'you must drink of the

Imrat of the sword.' 'O Guru,' replied Dalla, 'that which you have cut with a knife, is in effect the same.' The Guru was highly pleased with this answer, but still said, that he would be more fully satisfied if Dalla drank of the Imrat. 'That is perfectly true,' replied Dalla, falling at the Guru's feet. The next day after preparing Karah Pershad, he drank the Imrat, and distributed bhung to a hundred Seikhs. This so pleased the Guru, that he presented Dalla with a sword, a shield, and bangles studded with precious stones worth 2,000 rupees, together with a cloak. 'These I will not wear,' said Dalla, 'I will only worship them.'

One day a refugee arrived and informed the Guru that the Mahomedans were approaching. Dalla Singh armed himself and his soldiers for battle. 'We may have to fight these Mahomedans,' said he, 'and you will see how the Burars use their swords.'

Sakhi 103.

One day Ram Singh, the son of Phul, and Tiloka Singh, his brother, brought a great quantity of provisions in carts, as a present from Phul to the Guru. 'Have you brought this from your own houses?' asked the Guru. 'Yes,' replied Ram Singh and Tiloka Singh, 'we have brought all we had, as well as contributions of a maund or two a head from our town fellows.' Some Seikhs belonging to the Guru's household, said, 'These are the men who performed the funeral ceremonies of your sons, and mourned for them with true parental sorrow.' Another said, 'They waited on you at Kanghur, and paid their respects.' The Guru offered to give them anything they desired; and they being at that time of a nomad tribe, said, 'O Guru, we have never had a fixed abode in this world.' 'You shall soon have what you desire,' said the Guru, 'and your estates will descend to your heirs, generation after generation.'

He was very gracious to the men of Delhi and Lahore, and after presenting turbans to Ram Singh, and Tiloka Singh, told them that their dominions would extend from the mountains to Attock. They attended on the Guru for seven days, and then went home.

Sakhi 104.

When the Guru sent men to Bungara, to bring him a buffalo, the zamindars pointed out a vicious animal with the view of seeing some fun. The animal was scrubbing himself against a jand tree, as has been already stated. 'Come my good fellow,' said the Seikhs, 'let us release you from your sufferings.' As the buffalo made no resistance, the Bungarians began to think that it would be necessary to go and solicit the Guru's forgiveness for the offence they had contemplated. With this object they at length set out taking provisions, two guns, and some ruprees with them. The Guru was highly pleased with the guns and ruprees, but, at the same time, censured their conduct in connection with the buffalo. They admitted their fault, and the Guru was pleased to forgive them; but when they desired to have estates conferred upon them, as had been conferred upon Ram Singh, and Tiloka Singh, he said, 'As you have come to me, you shall retain the estates which you now hold a little time longer.'

SAKHI 105.

Ten days before starting for the Deccan, and while making his arrangements, the Guru sang a verse to the following effect: 'Myriads of Seikhs from the surrounding countries have come to see me.' His followers listened attentively. One at a time they approached to look at their Guru, and being filled with joy, simultaneously saluted him. Among those present were Dhurm Singh from Bhai Roha, Boodoo and Siddoo, the Dewanas, Abhai Ram Sohdi from Kotha, Dan Singh, and his son Gur Baksh Singh from Abloo Muniah, Bhai Mani Singh from Amritsar with all his followers, Bhai Ram Singh, and Bhai Dyal Singh from the village of Chak, Ram Singh and Tiloka Singh from Phul, and Bhai Goduria from Bhuchoo. All worshipped the Guru, and presented the gifts they had brought. The Guru's secretaries ventured to say, 'O King, you hold durbars here, and give audience to your friends and disciples, why then think of a journey to the barren countries of the Deccan?' 'I have business,' replied the Guru, 'and must go, though no doubt there is no better place than this dumdama.' After some friendly words with Ram Singh and Tiloka Singh, he dismissed them with khillats. To Bhai Ram Singh, and Bhai Dyal Singh he also gave khillats.

Bhai Gur Baksh Singh, Bhai Mani Singh, Bhai Dharm Singh, and Dan Singh's son, Gur Baksh Singh, and Bhai Suntokh Singh mounted their horses to accompany the Guru, but his servants and durbaris ran away that night with the Burars. Shodi Ava Singh, a man in whom the Guru placed great confidence, was carried along on his bed while asleep by Siddoo and Boodoo, the Dewanas ; and the Guru started himself, after performing some ceremonies at the shrine of the 9th Padsha, Tegh Bahadar, who had sojourned at this place 9 days. Guru Gobind Singh remained here exactly 9 months, 9 days, 9 pahars, and 9 minutes. He left on Monday the 5th Katik, at 10 o'clock in the morning.

SAKHI 106.

He encamped that day at Kaval which was 7 cos from the Dumdama.

SAKHI 107.

The next day at 12 o'clock he encamped at Jharer.

SAKHI 108.

The day after he pitched his tents at Jhanda, 18 cos from Jharar.

SAKHI 109.

While encamped 12 miles from Sirsa, after some conversation with Dalla, who sat on the ground near his bed, the Guru went to a brick-kiln, and calling to Dalla, said, 'Come I will shew you the estates I have promised you.' 'We will wait, and see them when we go there,' said Dalla, quietly putting in a pair of bangles, and a sword under the Guru's bedding. After walking twice round the camp that night, Dalla went home ; but no one saw him going except a Dewana faqir, who was himself walking round the camp at the time. The Guru called for Dalla about an hour and a half before sunrise, and the Dewana said, 'There is no Dalla or Mallah here, only Allah is present, for Dalla has run away.' 'For the last three births,' said the Guru, 'Dalla has always been with me. Is this the Dalla who wanted a seat to be always reserved for him at my side? How has he now left me of his own accord?'

Dalla had always objected to go to the Deccan and had also advised the Guru to remain where he was. The Guru was very anxious to take him, but Dalla always pleaded that there would be no one to look after his people in his absence. To meet his objection the Guru invariably said, 'You are not the only protector they have.'

Sakhi 110.

The Guru next encamped 12 cos further on at Nowhar, in the bed of a dry tank. 'Nowhar,' said he, 'shall be mine, and the Khalsa shall get mohurs here

hadara. Seeing a large jund tree, the Guru said, that the dominion of the Khalsa would begin when a peepul grew up near that tree, and destroyed it.

Sakhi 112.

The Sakhi of Suhawa, where the Guru has a shrine.

A man named Dowlat Ram, who had been expelled by Raja Karn Singh from Suhawa, took up his abode at Goori, but hearing that the Guru had come to his Dumdama, and that he possessed supernatural powers, being in fact an Avatar, he waited upon him. When asked why he had come, he said, 'Raja Karn Singh has expelled me from my home, and I have come to ask your protection.' 'Go home,' said the Guru, 'I will follow you.' Dowlat Ram accordingly went home.

Dalla's sister-in-law represented to the Guru that she had something to say. 'What is it,' enquired the Guru. 'I have,' she replied, 'killed my little girl, and feel that the sin will cling to me for ages, unless you graciously forgive me.' As the Guru gave her no answer, she asked the attendants what would propitiate him. Being told that he showed special favor to those who looked after his horses, she began to work in his stables from that day.

At Sirsa after drinking bhung, he mounted his horse for exercise, and riding to the top of a brick-kiln, asked which side the Deccan was, adding, after looking round, 'Look, it is close enough.'

Seeing a Seikh woman in his stables a short time after, he enquired who she was, and ordered her to be called. When she came he asked her why she was going about among his horses. She said, as before, that, having killed her daughter, she felt great remorse, and desired pardon. The Guru again made no reply.

He remained some days at Sirsa, whence be proceeded to Nowhar, where he halted several days. Starting from Nowhar, he next drank bhung at Sooharpur.

While he was encamped at Suhawa, Dowlat Ram and his four sons came to pay their respects. Being asked how many sons he had, Dowlat Ram said he had five. 'Where then is the fifth,' said the Guru. 'He must be somewhere here,' replied Dowlat Ram, 'he is mad.' 'He is not mad,' said the Guru, 'he is sane, and understands every thing. Call him.' He came and saluted the Guru, who, on hearing that his name was Boola, said, 'Call him Lall Singh, not Boola, for he is the only Lal (ruby) in your family. He will be the king of this country, and will support his brothers.'

Dhurm Singh, and Param Singh, the sons of the Bhai Rupa, made a bed for the Guru, and presented it to him. The Guru was very much pleased with it, and gave them, in return, a book containing 64 Sakhis or tales. The Guru happened to look towards his horses just at this moment, and seeing the Seikh woman again, asked who she was, and sent for her. She came, and began to flatter him. 'Why have you come to my camp,' said he. 'I am suffering from remorse,' she replied, 'for killing my daughter, and have come to solicit pardon, for without it, I shall suffer for 1,000 births.' The king after a short silence, told her to walk into the adjoining tank, dressed as she was. When the water came up to her mouth, the Guru ordered her to come out, telling her that her sins had been pardoned. He then told his disciples that in future all women guilty of a similar offence, would be pardoned on plunging into that tank in full dress.

As the Guru was undressing, a small snake about three inches in length, fell out of his waistband. The Seikhs tried to kill it, but it crawled away, and disappeared in a jund tree. They asked what this signified, and the Guru said, 'This snake was famine. I caught it in this Malwa, and intended to let it loose in the Malwa of Oojein, but it has escaped. Is there a Brhimma (a peepul tree) anywhere here?' The Seikhs searched throughout the jund forest, but could not find a peepul anywhere, till a man climbed the jund tree into which the snake had escaped, and found one about three inches long growing on it. 'This is Brhimma, not a peepul,' said the Guru, 'for the peepul is a symbol of Brhimma. This peepul is pervaded in a special manner with Brhimma's power, just as the incarnation of Khrishna is a special manifestation of Bhugwan. This jund is a demon, and this peepul a god. The god will overwhelm the demon. When I visit the Panjab the Khalsa will draw their swords. They shall become more formidable daily, and shall establish themselves in all quarters.'

In the meantime the brothers, Dowlat Ram and Fatta, came in and saluted the Guru, who immediately ordered bhung to be prepared and passed round; but Fatta refused to drink. The Guru pressed him, but he still refused, saying that he would become mad if he drank it. Dowlat Ram, however, drank; and the brothers after a little while returned home.

An old woman, named Bhawali, now came in, and presented a vessel of milk. Seeing a girl in her arms, the Guru asked how the child was related to her. 'She is my daughter,' said the old woman. 'Her daughter's son,' said the Guru, 'shall be my Seikh, and withal a very valiant man, and a great general, before whom no enemy shall be able to stand.'

Dowlat Ram and Fatta having reached home,

people began to remark that the former had taken bhung, while the latter had refused it, and asked the reason why. Fatta said that he was willing to take it now. He accordingly again presented himself before the Guru, and asked for bhung, but was told that Dowlat Ram had drunk it all. 'There is some unprepared bhung,' said the Guru, 'prepare it for yourself.' 'Let me have that even,' said Fatta. They gave him the dregs of the last potation, and whatever could be got by washing the pestle and the strainers, he drank it and became intoxicated.

The Guru spoke very graciously to Dalla, and again requested that he would accompany him to the Deccan, promising to confer a sovereignty upon him. 'I am,' said Dalla, 'the ruler of this country. It will be better to leave me where I am.' 'No,' said the Guru, 'you must accompany me. Nowranga (Aurangzebe) is dead, and the throne of Delhi is vacant; come with me, and I will place you on it.' 'I am,' said Dalla, 'a keeper of cows, better leave me here.' 'No,' said the Guru, 'come with me. Wherever I am, a seat shall be reserved for you.'

'The marauders,' expostulated Dalla, 'will devastate the country. I am its protector, leave me here.' 'Go then,' said the Guru, 'the country shall be saved, but you shall perish.'

Ram Singh and Tiloka Singh, clasping their hands, said, 'Command us, and we will accompany you to the Deccan.' 'I have,' said the Guru, 'conferred on you the sovereignty of this country.' As it was now getting dark, Dalla and the other courtiers hastened to their homes. Next morning the Guru enquired after them, and a Malang faqir replied, 'All have gone, Dalla as well as Mullah. There are neither courtiers nor servants; no one, in fact, save Allah.'

Dowlat Ram now came in and presented a Khase (sheet) to the Guru, who said, 'He who has a Khase, shall also have the Dase (country); your offspring shall rule for five generations, and then my Khalsa shall reign.'

He then ordered his attendants to prepare Karah Pershad. 'Take,' said he, '5 rupees and 4 annas with you. Give 4 annas to the bania as profit, and bring exactly five rupees worth of materials.' The Seikhs went, and asked for the materials required, offering four annas as profit. The bania, however, only gave them four rupees worth, saying, 'I have given you five rupees worth of things, and have taken four annas as profit.' When the things were brought before the Guru, he asked how much they had spent. They stated that they had bought 5 rupees worth of things, and had given 4 annas as profit. 'Why have you brought only 4 Rs. worth?' said the Guru; 'go and call the bania.' He was accordingly called, and being asked how many rupees worth of things he had given, said, 'I have given 5 Rs. worth, and taken 4 annas as profit.' 'Why, you have given only 4 Rs. worth,' said the Guru. The bania clasped his hands, and fell at the Guru's feet, who made him restore the amount he had taken fraudulently fourfold. Karah Pershad was now prepared; and the bania was converted to Seikhism. After the feast the Guru ordered the Seikhs to return to their families in the Panjab, conjuring them to remain firm in their faith. He himself set out for the Deccan, on the 5th Kathie, when the moon was in her second quarter.

Here ends the Sakhi. Say 'Wah Guru, brothers.' He who reads this attentively shall obtain the Guru's blessing.

Sakhi 113.

The Guru then encamped at Madhusedhana, 18 miles further on.

Sakhi 114.

The Guru next marched 18 miles, and encamped at Puhkar.

Sakhi 115.

He next encamped at Churn.

Sakhi 116.

The Guru next pitched his tents at Naraina, near the mausoleum of Dadoo. He saluted the mausoleum by lifting an arrow to his head, and the Khalsa demanded a fine, which he immediately offered to pay. The Khalsa having fixed the fine at Rs. 5,000, a Seikh objected that it was too much, and proposed to reduce it to Rs. 500. Another thinking Rs. 500 too much, some one said, that the Guru would not feel the loss of that sum. One, however, said that he would not be satisfied under five lakhs; but it was argued, that, though the Guru could pay even that sum, still the Khalsa would find it impossible to pay fines in proportion hereafter. They at length asked the Guru to pay Rs. 125, which they spent in the purchase of a kitchen tent for the Guru's followers. The Sadoo in charge of the mausoleum was a pupil of Dadoo's pupil. Several Seikhs visited him, and when he asked who the Guru was, told him that he was Guru Gobind Singh, who had succeeded Guru Nanak Jee; that he was at war with the King of Delhi, and had contended with him for 8 months, during which period he had taken ten lakhs of horses; and that he was now returning. They also described the battle in which the Guru had defeated the Mahomedans. Hearing all this, the Mahanth rose to go and pay his respects to the Guru, but the Sadoo advised, that he should be sent for. The Mahanth was of opinion that it was always proper to go to one who was so supremely great, and withal a visitor, to whom deference is always due. Taking some sweetmeats, and accompanied by other Sadoos, he set out to wait on the Guru, whom he found seated on a platform at the foot of a bir tree. After the usual greetings, the Guru said, 'Come, be seated, O disciples of Dadoo.' 'This war,' said the chief Sadoo, 'is to support the claims you have advanced. Your ancestors never asserted such claims.' 'No,' said the Guru, 'he who would lift a brick to throw at a man, had better take a stone. The Mahomedans have grievously persecuted devotees, faqirs and Brahmans, and we must therefore root them out.' When the Sadoos brought provisions for the Guru's kitchen, he asked them to provide flesh also for his falcons, but the Sadoos requested that he would give them grain instead that day. 'Give it to them,' said the Guru, 'if they will eat it.' The falcons got some 'jawar' which they ate.

SAKHI 117.

The Guru encamped next at Lali, a place 25 cos further on.

SAKHI 118.

The Guru next halted at Mugrowda, which is 25 cos from Lali.

SAKHI 119.

The next day he pitched his camp at Kalaith, 25 cos from Mugrowda, and halted there ten days. May the true Guru help us.

SAKHI 120.

Or the Sakhi of Swaithsur (the white lake).

While encamped at Jussi, the Guru and his followers plunged in the lake, mounted and accoutred, and crossed over to the other side. The Guru's horse, which was black, turned white, except about the head; and the Guru's robes also turned white, the turban only retaining its original colour. He changed his dress on the opposite bank, and the

Seikhs in astonishment enquired what all this meant. 'You plunged into the lake mounted,' said they, 'and your horse, and your robes have turned white!' 'This is a sacred bathing place,' replied the Guru, 'and this is the auspicious hour. Ram Chander Jee in ancient times, when he was at war with his sons Love, and Kush, stopped at this lake, on his return from Ram Teerath.' The Seikhs then began to bathe in the lake, the Guru having told them that it was the auspicious hour, and the time of the Avijit Nakshatar. 'This lake,' continued the Guru, 'washes away the sins of those who bathe in it. The horse's head will shew that he was entirely black before; and you will also be reminded that I was on my way to the Deccan when the change took place. The Seikhs will hereafter say, that they were journeying to the Deccan when the Guru's horse turned white. The turban I kept black to make the Nihang Seikhs adopt that color. Rama Nand performed penance here.' The Seikhs reminded him, that Rama Nand was born at Kashi, but he said, 'There were two

Rama Nands. Rama Nand of Kashi was the head of the Bhagats, and the other was a follower of Nirad. He was first called Ahlee, and used to look after cattle. He was born in a village, which is now lying in ruins in the midst of the wild tract of country surrounding Bathinda and Ramanwal. While grazing his cows he met Nirad, who taught him his devotions, and placing his hands on his head, inspired him with knowledge to discern between right and wrong, saying, 'He who calls you Ahlee, shall meet with disasters, but he who calls you Rama Nand shall obtain happiness.' His cows returned to their village, but he came at once to Swaithsur, to perform penance; and yonder is his mausoleum.' The Seikhs asked which was the best day for bathing, and the Guru told them that it would be best to bathe when the sun is entering the tenth sign of the zodiac.

Ram Chander Jee pitched his camp under a clump of Phulai trees to the west of Swaithsur, the traditions regarding which are well known throughout the country of Malwa.

A cloud of dust was seen in the direction of Phulloo, and the Seikhs concluded, that a Mahomedan army was approaching, but the Guru said, that it was only caused by some of his followers who were coming to see him. A party was sent out to reconnoitre, and they found on enquiry, that the followers of Lawana Seikh were approaching. On being asked who was encamped near the lake, they said that it was Guru Gobind Singh, the true king. They came back, and made their report. Lawana shortly after waited upon the Guru, and after making his obeisance, presented 30 maunds of jaggery, which was distributed to the Seikhs and the horses. Lawana Singh used to give a tenth of his annual income to the Guru.

Two Jogis came and stood on the west bank of the lake, and saluted the Guru, who made signs of welcome to them. Holding up one of his fingers, and then two, and so on in succession, he at last laid his open hand on his bosom. The Jogis went away evidently satisfied, but the Seikhs protested against this proceeding by reminding the

Guru, that it was his order not to have any intercourse with those who pierced their ears. 'They were Gopi Chand, and Bhatri,' said the Guru. 'Let us then,' said the Seikhs, 'pay our respects to them.' 'They are in the Lal Bazar at Delhi,' rejoined the Guru. 'Pray explain,' demanded the Seikhs, 'what you meant by the signs you made.' 'The Jogis,' replied the Guru, 'represented that the present age was a very trying one, that the Rakiswars, Monishwars, and Sidhs had left the world in alarm; and asked how I would manage with the multitude I had collected round me. I replied by holding up one finger, to indicate, that by ministering to even one Seikh, it would be possible to overcome the difficulties of life. They suggested that the Seikhs might not be sufficiently pure and virtuous to enable me to overcome the evils of the world. I then held up two fingers. When they made further objections, I held up all my fingers. They still had doubts, however, and said, 'The times are hard. Suppose, that, even after ministering to five Seikhs, we should fail.' I then placed my open hand on my breast, to imply, that, he who ministered to five Seikhs, would be under my special protection, and that I would be his patron. They then admitted, that under those circumstances, there would be nothing to fear.'

The Guru halted nearly 10 days at Jassi, and the people of the village showed him every attention. He stayed exactly 9 days, 9 pahars, 9 hours, and 9 minutes. When he was leaving, the villagers made offerings to him, according to their means.

Here end the Sakhis. Praise be to the Guru.

FINIS.